Rock Creek Park

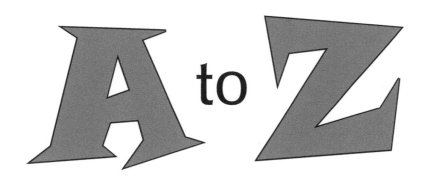

A to Z

An alphabetical account
of the natural wonders
and historical surprises
in the wildest part
of Washington, DC

David Swerdloff
and
Lorraine Swerdloff

Design: Lorraine Swerdloff

ISBN 978-0-692-59408-7

Front cover (clockwise from top): Boulder Bridge (Carol M. Highsmith, 2010): Library of Congress; Theodore Roosevelt on horseback jumping over a split rail fence (1902): LOC; Hairy woodpecker: Matthew Sileo/matthewsileophotography.com; Detail of Indian—Q Street Bridge (Jack E. Boucher, 1993): LOC; Blagden Mill ruins, 1890s: National Park Service; Deer in Rock Creek Park, Matthew Sileo/matthew-sileophotography.com.

Back cover (clockwise from top): Rocks in Rock Creek: Lorraine Swerdloff; Joaquin Miller Cabin (DB King, 2005): via flickr.com, cropped, Creative Commons 2.0 license; Volkswagen in Milkhouse Ford (9/26/1965): NPS; Fawn drawn by President Theodore Roosevelt: *Theodore Roosevelt's Letters to His Children*, Charles Scribner's Sons, 1919; White-breasted nuthatch in Rock Creek Park, Matthew Sileo/matthew-sileophotography.com; Taft Memorial Bridge, Isometric Cutaway (Ann Wheaton, 1995): LOC; Gizzard Shad: Brian Gratwicke/DCNature.com, Creative Commons 2.5 license; Detail from Contrabands at Camp Brightwood in 2nd R.I. Camp (1861): LOC; Detail from Chieftain of Virginia (engraving by Theodor de Bry after watercolor by John White, 1590): LOC.

Facing page: Rock Creek (2008): Brian Gratwicke/DCNature.com, Creative Commons 2.5 license.

Amazing stories accompany every twist and turn of Rock Creek.

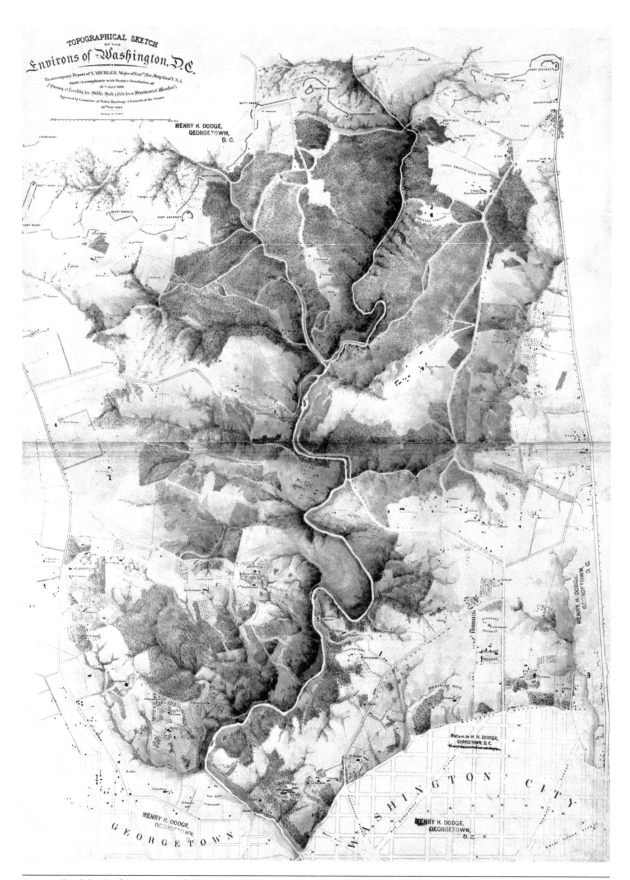

Topographical sketch of the environs of Washington, DC (Nathaniel Michler, 1867): Library of Congress; Park sign (opposite): David Swerdloff.

Foreword

When we visit National Parks around the country, we like to tell park rangers we live next door to a National Park in Washington, DC. That usually leaves them puzzled. What park could that be?

Rock Creek Park seems to be Washington's secret. One of the nation's pioneering urban parks, Rock Creek is a haven for hikers and history buffs, birders and bicyclists. Only two National Parks were declared before Rock Creek Park was established in 1890. Yet few Americans are aware that, in the words of naturalist John Burroughs, their capital city "has on its very threshold so much natural beauty and grandeur, such as men seek for in remote forests and mountains."

Each alphabetical entry in this book began as part of a weekly blog during the park's 125th anniversary year, 2015, posted on the Rock Creek Conservancy's website. The Conservancy is focused on protecting and enhancing Rock Creek Park in partnership with government agencies, nonprofits, and local businesses, communities and residents.

We are grateful to the Conservancy's Margo Reid and Paul Mufarrij for their help with the blog — and encourage readers to generously support RCC. Special thanks also go out to wildlife photographer Matthew Sileo for his stunning images and to Melanie Choukas-Bradley, author of *A Year in Rock Creek Park,* for her advice and for the nature hikes she leads.

A good starting point for any discussion of Rock Creek Park is the map on the facing page prepared in 1867 by Major Nathanial Michler of the US Army Corps of Engineers. Called on by Congress to search for a possible site for a new White House, he was so awestruck by Rock Creek Valley that his report stressed instead its preservation as parkland.

Rock Creek Park has indeed been preserved as a wild woodland in the heart of DC. When you're not there making new discoveries with every step, read a page or two here and learn a little more with every letter.

David and Lorraine Swerdloff

A is for **Animals**

Red fox

With its forest, water and meadow habitats, Rock Creek Park is home to a wide variety of creatures. Over time, they have ranged from ancient mastodons and Colonial Era bison to recent coyote sightings.

For its first human visitors, Rock Creek was not quite a Jurassic Park. But the ancient American Indians who camped in the area did hunt big game ranging from mammoths, mastodons and musk oxen to caribou, wolves, beavers, lynx, moose and black bears.

Early colonial settler Henry Fleet wrote in 1631, "As for deer, buffaloes [sic], bears, turkeys, the woods do swarm with them." As more people came to the Rock Creek Valley to live and establish farms and mills, many species declined or disappeared. By the late 1800s, Thomas Blagden — one of the valley's primary landowners — fenced in 20 or 30 acres to create a "deer park." The does and bucks he raised were by then such a novelty that Washingtonians rode up from "the city" to see them.

Unlike the deer, those bears and bison have yet to make a comeback along Rock Creek — except at the National Zoo. But hundreds of species of animals are now at home inside the city thanks to the Park's protected habitat.

The forests provide shelter, food and nesting sites for numerous bird, reptile and mammal species. The woodlands shade the wetlands, keeping the water cool and welcoming to amphibian communities. Tree branches provide an important resting spot for tropical birds heading south for the winter or flying north to breeding grounds. Meadows and recreation areas supply habitats for other animals and insects.

Meet Your Mammals

Today, 30 species of mammals live inside the Park, most commonly whitetail deer, raccoons, red and gray foxes, squirrels, chipmunks, shrews, moles, voles, mice, rabbits, beavers and — since their first confirmed sighting in 2004 — coyotes.

The presence of coyotes provides another reason to follow Park regulations and keep your dog on a leash. But we can also thank these newcomers for eating a lot of rats and mice — and they may help the Park's own conservation efforts aimed at decreasing the deer population from today's dangerous levels.

A white-tailed buck on the edge of Rock Creek Park rubs against shrubs to remove the velvet from his antlers.

The deer are eating so many tree seedlings and feasting on so much of the understory of non-woody plants that the native forests can't regenerate, the environment is losing its native shrubs and wildflowers, and other animal species are finding their habitats greatly reduced.

Another notable Park mammal is the black squirrel (right). While no zoo today would release non-native species into the surrounding environment, the black squirrels we see scampering throughout the Washington, DC area are all descendants of a small group of Canadian squirrels housed at the National Zoo and let out on purpose in the early 1900s.

Creepers and Swimmers

The Park's most familiar reptile species include various snakes, turtles, skinks and lizards. The most common amphibian is the red-backed salamander. There are also more than 160 species of birds living in or migrating through the park, and nearly three dozen varieties of fish.

You should be seeing those fish in greater numbers now that they can reach spawning grounds upstream. Carefully placed boulders have created natural-looking rapids that allow fish to swim beyond sewer pipes and other obstacles. And the concrete fish ladder that opened in 2007 helps herring, shad, alewives, striped bass and other species get around the old ornamental waterfall at Peirce Mill. Perhaps Rock Creek will again experience the massive spring fish migrations of centuries past.

The Eastern painted turtle is one of four common turtle species found in the Park, along with the Eastern box turtle, snapping turtle and red-eared slider.

Rock Creek Park still contains several dozen seeps and springs, the remnants of a larger system that used to provide the city with much of its best drinking water. These freshwater habitats offer a home to some rare animals, including the only endangered species believed to live in the Park. The Hay's Spring amphipod is an eyeless, colorless crustacean less than an inch long that looks like a shrimp.

Sights and Sounds

Some of the Park's greatest pleasures come from witnessing wildlife — seeing the red streak of a fox running across your path, viewing fish from the bank of the creek, happening upon a painted turtle or wood frog. Other joys come from noticing the sounds of birds calling to each other, the rat-a-tat of woodpeckers boring into tree trunks, the chirps and cadences of crickets and cicadas.

The Barred Owl flies through Park forests and swoops down on its prey, including small mammals and birds.

An event in May 2007 focused on experiencing as many of the animal (and plant) species as possible in a single 24-hour period. BioBlitz, sponsored by the National Park Service and National Geographic, offered a snapshot of the rich variety of life in Rock Creek Park. Volunteer naturalists hurried to identify as many species as possible in just a day, counting more than 650 different kinds of plants and animals. The total included 15 species of mammals, 82 kinds of birds, 23 fishes, 15 amphibians and reptiles, 16 aquatic invertebrates, 28 terrestrial invertebrates and 154 insects.

How many can you find during your next trip down a Rock Creek trail?

Buck, Turtle, Owl: Matthew Sileo/MatthewSileoPhotography.com. Fox, Squirrel: Wikimedia Commons.

B is for Bridges

Rock Creek Valley is not the Grand Canyon. But don't underestimate the challenge of building bridges from one side to the other.

The **Taft Bridge** (above), more than 900 feet long, was one of America's first cast concrete bridges and remains one of the world's largest unreinforced concrete structures. Completed in 1907 as the Connecticut Avenue Bridge, it was so expensive that Washingtonians commonly called it the Million Dollar Bridge before the span was renamed for William Howard Taft in 1931.

1906 · SIXTEENTH STREET BRIDGE · 1910
OVER PINEY BRANCH PARKWAY
WASHINGTON, D.C.

ELEVATION/SECTION

PLAN

SITE LOCATION

Washington, D.C.

The **Dumbarton** (or **Q Street) Bridge**, finished in 1915, was built with a gentle curve so the span could connect Georgetown with the Dupont Circle area. Construction crews also had to cope with a big obstacle directly between Q Street in Georgetown and the west end of the bridge: the Dumbarton House mansion. The house was moved 100 feet north of its original location.

It took the completion of the **16th Street Bridge** over Piney Branch in 1910 for development to reach many of the neighborhoods north of Mount Pleasant. [Note to bridge geeks: this span is considered the first parabolic concrete arch in the United States.]

Lions and Tigers and Bison – Oh My!

These larger bridges were often beautifully adorned. The **Taft Bridge** is guarded by four bronze lions, with iron eagles taking flight from the lampposts. The limestone **Duke Ellington Bridge**, built in 1935 as the Calvert Street Bridge, features four sculptural reliefs alongside its three graceful arches; each relief represents a different mode of travel: auto, train, ship and airplane.

Sculptor Alexander Phimister Proctor created the massive bronze bison (right) on the **Q Street Bridge** (as well as bison keystones on Memorial Bridge and two bison heads in the State Dining Room at the White House). He was originally hired to sculpt four bison for the **16th Street Bridge** as well. Believing they would be too expensive, he came up with a cheaper alternative: a quartet of tigers.

The **Q Street Bridge** also features sandstone busts (left) of an American Indian chief, taken from a life mask of Kicking Bear, a Lakota Sioux who fought alongside his cousin, Crazy Horse.

Man-Size Rocks

Boulder Bridge (left) has been the iconic image of Rock Creek Park nearly from the time it replaced an older plank bridge in 1902. As the story is told, the designer called for "man-size" boulders — meaning rocks big enough for a man to handle on his own. But the message was misinterpreted, with workers bringing in boulders nearly the size of a man. Theodore Roosevelt is credited with naming the span when he placed a classified ad in the *Evening Star* in 1902 looking for a gold ring he lost "100 yards above boulder bridge." Just south of the bridge, you can still see stone supports for a late 19th century span that took the old Blagden's Mill Road across the creek.

The **Ross Drive Bridge** (left, built in 1907), a half-mile south of Joyce Road, was listed in the National Register of Historic Places in 1979 at the same time as Boulder Bridge. For engineering fans, the National Park Service points out that it is "one of the earliest known triple-hinge bridges in the United States." For those of us just enjoying the view, we can agree with the NPS that the columns "complement the deep ravine and add to the quality of the setting."

Many of the footbridges found in the park today were constructed by New Deal workers during the 1930s — including **Bluff Bridge, Boundary Bridge, Rapids Bridge, Riley Springs Bridge** and **Rolling Meadows Bridge.**

The park's oldest bridge is the 1872 span across the creek at **Peirce Mill**, although it has been significantly renovated over the years.

Bygone Bridges

One of the park's prettiest bridges stood for only about 60 years. The **Pebble Dash Bridge** (right, built in 1902) took Beach Drive over Broad Branch creek. Just east of the bridge, travelers had to depend on a ford to cross Rock Creek. When the ford was removed in the 1960s, the bridge was torn down so the entire intersection could be rebuilt.

There's a good reason why cyclists have to duck when riding the path under the **Pennsylvania Avenue Bridge**. The original 1860 span (below) was renowned for its low arch, formed by a pair of cast-iron pipes. These four-foot-wide water mains supported the bridge, even as they served as part of a system of reservoirs, tunnels and pipes that brought water into Washington from Great Falls. The current span constructed in 1916 retained the silhouette — and those iron pipes are still there, imbedded in concrete.

B is also for Birds

Only a healthy habitat can sustain our resident swallows, chickadees and (as the old song puts it) every little bird in the tall oak tree.

To experience one of the park's natural wonders, take a walk through the woods just after dawn in late April and early May. Dozens of species of songbirds are arriving during their spring migration, dressed in their most brilliant plumage and trilling their sweetest songs. As Rock Creek rambles for more than 32 miles from upper Montgomery County to the Potomac River, the green parkland along its banks marks the path of the Atlantic Flyway for these birds that winter in the tropics.

Binoculars in hand, birders seeking good vantage points can often be found along the Western Ridge trail between Broad Branch and Military Road, especially near the Nature Center and maintenance yard. Later in the day, the warblers, vireos, tanagers and thrushes scatter through the forest to feed and rest, making them harder to spot.

Dozens of migrating species make the park their summer home. The list includes many LBBs (little brown birds), who often make up for their drab colors with lovely calls. But the roster is also enlivened by richly hued wood ducks, ruby-throated hummingbirds, yellow-breasted chats and purple martins. During breeding season, some males — like scarlet tanagers and indigo buntings — practically scream with color. Dozens more migratory species wing their way further north to breeding grounds as distant as the Arctic. Park visitors celebrate all of these avian travelers each May during Migratory Bird Day festivities.

Later in the year, these bird populations reassemble along Rock Creek during the fall migration. But, since they no longer have to impress potential mates, they may appear with more muted melodies and duller or molting feathers.

The National Zoo is transforming the exhibit space around its historic 1928 Bird House into "Experience Migration," a collection of aviaries and research areas focusing on migratory birds of the Americas. In addition to its collection of captive birds, the Zoo attracts many wild species, including a notable warm-weather colony of black-crowned night herons.

Two of the more uncommon migratory species spotted in the park during the autumn and winter are the Cooper's hawk and ruby-crowned kinglet.

Arriving in the spring migration are such birds as the Eastern phoebe and (shown devouring an insect) blue-gray gnatcatcher. Above, a black-crowned night heron takes its place as part of a celebrated colony nesting each spring near the Bird House at the National Zoo.

The great blue heron (left) may benefit from improved water quality and increasing fish populations in Rock Creek. Among the familiar species found in the park year-round are (right) the red-bellied woodpecker, Northern cardinal and blue jay, and (top of previous page) the American robin.

Permanent Residents

Rock Creek Park's rich landscape also sustains many year-round populations that take advantage of the resources of the forests, meadows, floodplains and the creek itself. In any season, the park can echo with the rat-a-tat of a woodpecker, the hoot of an owl or the chatter of a kingfisher. Some of these resident birds are so common that Washingtonians may take their distinctive shades for granted: from blue jays and red-breasted robins to the vivid hues of male cardinals, mallards and goldfinches.

Winters are also brightened by red-tailed hawks, dark-eyed juncos, yellow-bellied sapsuckers and other species that arrive in the fall and depart in the spring. One of the most common cold-weather visitors, the white-throated sparrow, has a distinctive call sometimes described as "Poor Sam Peabody, Peabody, Peabody."

Birds in Peril

In the space of a half-century, about 70 percent fewer migratory songbirds are coming to breed in Rock Creek Park. Some of the decline can be traced to deforestation and other ecological problems in their Latin American wintering grounds. But the Rock Creek environment provides its own challenges. Predators like raccoons, possums and other birds keep many species from nesting. Large numbers of deer eat away the understory plants that provide homes, food and cover for many birds — and, as they browse on tree seedlings, they are altering the composition of the forest.

The National Audubon Society has identified climate change as the number one threat to birds. Their 2014 study took data from decades of winter and summer bird counts across America and correlated those numbers with detailed temperature and precipitation readings. The result was a series of maps revealing how predicted changes in climate might modify the summer and winter ranges of nearly 600 kinds of birds. According to the models, one in five species would lose more than half their current range by 2050.

The maps indicate that some of Rock Creek Park's iconic birds are at risk. Future summers may lack the flash of red from the scarlet tanager, the bright orange of the Baltimore oriole and the flute-like song of DC's official bird, the wood thrush. The common mallard may show up in the winter, but not summer. Hairy woodpeckers may become uncommon, especially in summer.

To help expand bird-friendly habitats, landscape with native plants and avoid pesticides and herbicides. Apply reflective decals to windows. Install birdhouses. Keep cats inside. Encourage building owners to turn off excess lighting that can disorient migrating species. Support programs like DC Audubon's Rock Creek Songbirds initiative, which plants trees and shrubs that sustain bird populations. Participate in the annual Christmas Bird Count each December.

Together we can ensure that our native birds continue to rock in the treetops all day long.

The wood thrush above was captured during the May 2007 BioBlitz—a 24-hour effort that identified more than 650 plant and animal species in Rock Creek Park, including 82 types of birds. The Rock Creek Songbirds project aims to protect iconic species like the wood thrush—DC's official bird—by planting trees and marking nesting sites (below, along the Soapstone Valley Trail).

American robins, Cooper's hawk, ruby-crowned kinglet, blue-gray gnat-catcher, Northern cardinal, blue jay: Matthew Sileo/MatthewSileoPhotography.com; great blue heron: Carol M. Highsmith Archive, Library of Congress; black-crowned night heron (Brian Gratwicke 2006, cropped) and wood thrush (Ryan Valdez 2007, cropped): DCNature.com under Creative Commons 2.5 license; Eastern phoebe (Katja Schulz 2014, cropped) and red-bellied woodpecker (GlynLowe.com 2011, cropped): via flickr.com under Creative Commons 2.0 license; Bird Nesting sign: David Swerdloff. All birds photographed in Rock Creek Park or the National Zoo.

C is for Carter Barron

Many legendary performers played the Carter Barron Amphitheatre. But the stage was created to celebrate DC— and American— history.

Why was the Carter Barron Amphitheatre built? The biggest clue is found in the venue's original name, the Sesquicentennial Amphitheatre.

When the outdoor concert space opened in 1950 along Colorado Avenue NW, the object was to honor the 150th anniversary of the District of Columbia as America's capital city — and to do so by staging a historic pageant each summer.

Pulitzer Prize-winning dramatist Paul Green supplied a musical about the life of George Washington, titled *Faith of Our Fathers*. Green authored 15 similar "symphonic dramas," including *The Lost Colony*, which continues to be staged each summer in North Carolina.

Faith of Our Fathers had a short run in 1950 because of construction delays. The executive vice chairman of the National Capital Sesquicentennial Commission, Carter T. Barron, died that November, and the theater was renamed in his honor.

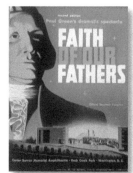

Following a less-than-stellar 1951 season, the pageant was not renewed — leaving authorities to ponder what to do with the outdoor theater. Despite neighborhood opposition to commercial uses of the space, outside promoters were allowed to stage nine ballet performances in 1952 and a 12-week program of Broadway musicals in 1953.

Bruce, Ella and the Ice Capades

As the years passed, Carter Barron featured an expanding roster of live entertainment. In the 1950s, performers included Benny Goodman, Louis Armstrong and Jimmy Durante. The 1955 production of the Ice Capades not only featured an ice rink that filled the stage, but the show was promoted with free sledding on some

25 tons of snow created one Sunday afternoon in August.

In the 1960s, audiences could enjoy jazz from Ella Fitzgerald and Stan Getz; folk from Peter, Paul and Mary, Odetta and the Kingston Trio; star turns by Ethel Merman and Harry Belafonte; nearly every legend of Motown; plus ballets, musicals, operas and the circus.

The amphitheatre was the first federally owned center for the performing arts — and, in

its early years, the only permanent outdoor theater of its kind in Washington. As a US government facility, it also stood out as one of the area's few integrated theater houses during the 1950s and into the 1960s.

By the mid-60s, new, more modern concert spaces were being built. Despite the amphitheatre's setting in a natural bowl shaded by the treetops of Rock Creek Park, fewer people were willing to attend shows in the middle of the city that could be interrupted at any time by wind and rain.

Still, three concerts by Bruce Springsteen demonstrated that, even in 1975, popular artists could fill the arena no matter what the weather, as an *Evening Star* review noted:

> Springsteen drew 4,300 people to the 4,100-seat Carter Barron Amphitheatre…. Last night's crowd had to sit through two torrential downpours that held up the show for nearly two hours…. None of this seemed to bother the audience. They cheered and yelled and stomped their feet as if they were in the comfort of the Capital Centre.

The National Park Service took over operation of the theater from private promoters after the 1976 season. One of its most successful partnerships was with the Shakespeare Theater, which provided free performances of Shakespeare plays each year from 1991 to 2008. Although the Carter Barron stage has seen fewer big-name acts in recent decades — and its infrastructure is in need of millions of dollars in repairs — Washingtonians can still enjoy summertime concerts under the stars.

Show Business' Ambassador to Washington

Beginning with his arrival in Washington in 1932, Carter T. Barron's job title was manager of the Eastern Division of Loew's Theaters. But this was the era when theater managers often served as community leaders — and Barron organized benefits, balls and fundraising drives for causes that ranged from the March of Dimes to war bonds.

When DC still had a reputation as a sleepy Southern town, he used his Hollywood connections to recruit the biggest names of stage, screen and radio to perform in Washington, participate in charity events and golf tournaments, and interact with political and civic leaders. Back in Hollywood, the moguls realized it was a good idea to get along with Presidents and politicos. As Barron connected the two worlds, he earned the title of Show Business' Ambassador to Washington.

It was his idea to mark the inauguration of the President by staging a star-studded variety show. He organized the first such gala in 1941 for Franklin Roosevelt, with a bill that included Irving Berlin, Mickey Rooney, Charlie Chaplin, Raymond Massey, Douglas Fairbanks Jr., Nelson Eddy and Ethel Barrymore.

Carter Barron naturally took the leading role in the Sesquicentennial Commission, which was officially headed by President Truman. Mr. Truman himself dedicated the Amphitheatre in Barron's honor, with actor Walter Pidgeon providing the eulogy.

President Truman (r) dedicating the amphitheatre to Carter T. Barron in front of a portrait of Mr. Barron, May 25, 1951: National Archives. 1965 season opening night crowd, June 14, 1965 (Abbie Rowe) and Carter Barron aerial photo, August 14, 1950: National Park Service. Show programs courtesy George Washington University Libraries Special Collections. *Evening Star* display ads reprinted with permission of the DC Public Library, *Star* Collection, ©*Washington Post*.

C also is for Civil Rights

When Rock Creek Park was established in 1890, DC's slaves had been emancipated for fewer than 30 years. The legacy of slavery and discrimination would not be easily erased.

America's ongoing struggle for racial equality is reflected in the history of Rock Creek Park.

Earlier in the 19th century, some free blacks lived in the rural countryside near Rock Creek, including a community founded in Brightwood in the 1830s. But many more residents of African descent suffered in bondage. As the most significant slave owners in the area, the Peirce family depended on enslaved blacks in their enterprises, including Peirce Mill.

After slaves in the nation's capital were freed in April 1862 — more than eight months before Abraham Lincoln signed the Emancipation Proclamation — scores of slaves who fled captivity in the South came to Washington to volunteer for the Union cause. Called "contrabands" because in Confederate eyes they represented valuable property, these poorly paid freedmen helped build and maintain the city's Civil War defenses. Many of them were based at Camp Brightwood, located close to Fort

Photograph shows two Union officers at Camp Brightwood with three African American "contrabands" — two men and a boy.

EMANCIPATION IN THE DISTRICT OF COLUMBIA.

A.—*List of the petitions filed, &c.*—Continued.

Name of petitioner or claimant.	Persons held to service or labor.			Total.	To whom paid
	No.	Names.	Value.		
Joshua Peirce............	10	Jeremiah Gibson......	306 60		
		Nancy Carroll	175 30		
		William H. Beckett..	569 40		
		Thomas Rhodes......	613 20		
		Anna M. Rustin......	436 00		
		Ellen Beckett........	595 60		
		Charlotte R. Carroll..	481 80		
		Anthony J. Carroll...	459 90		
		Charles J. Carroll...	43 80		
		Wm. Nicholas Rustin.	21 99		
				3, 635 40	Joshua Peirce.

The 1862 Act freeing DC's slaves allowed slave owners to apply for compensation. Congressional records documented the petition from Joshua Peirce, who relied on the labor of the slaves listed above to perform such jobs as nursery foreman, market salesman, housekeeper and horse expert.

Stevens. The fort itself was built on land owned by a free black named Elizabeth Proctor Thomas. Like many whose homesteads were seized for the war effort, "Aunt Betty" never received compensation.

The area's African American population surged after the war. With the opening of the National Zoo in 1891, Rock Creek Valley provided a gathering spot for black Washingtonians on the Monday after Easter. The enduring tradition may have started because, at the time, African Americans were barred from the White House Easter Egg Roll, yet many black workers had Easter Monday off.

DC's modern Emancipation Day holiday recalls the annual celebrations — such as this one depicted in 1866 — that marked the anniversary of the freeing of slaves in the District of Columbia on April 16, 1862.

Jim Crow Nests along Rock Creek

Before Rock Creek Park came under the authority of the National Park Service in 1933, some of the DC officials managing the park opposed integration. Army engineer Clarence

Sherrill — park supervisor from 1921 to 1925 — was rebuked in the African American press as "the same man who recently had posted signs in Rock Creek park segregating persons of Color, and also the same man who was in charge of the segregated seating arrangements at the dedication of the Lincoln Memorial" (*Chicago Defender* 8/5/1922).

Many unemployed African Americans were put to work during the 1930s by New Deal agencies, including this Civil Works Administration crew along Piney Branch Parkway.

The local chapter of the NAACP began protests in 1930 after discovering that many park picnic areas were still off-limits to black visitors. For three decades ending in the 1930s, only white children were admitted to Camp Goodwill, the park's summer haven for underprivileged kids. When the DC Recreation Board voted in 1945 to mandate segregation at District facilities — including those on federal land — the headline in the *Baltimore Afro-American* (6/23/1945) read: "Recreation Board Okeys Jim Crow – Eloquent Protest of Tan Member Ignored – Hate Boys Win 4-2." The Board changed its policy in 1949 only after an ultimatum from the Interior Department.

Even as late as 1964, Rock Creek Park was cited on the floor of the Senate as Hubert Humphrey made the case for landmark civil rights legislation:

> Mr. President, suppose you attempted to go into Rock Creek Park with your loved ones on Sunday, but discovered you first had to go to court for authority to use these public facilities? How long would most white citizens tolerate such a state of affairs? Is it any wonder that colored people demonstrate?

Unearthing Black History

Archeologists have studied the homesteads of several African Americans who lived in Rock Creek Park at the time of its founding.

The only black property owners were Jane Dickson and Charles Dickson. Each had a small house and garden on separate quarter-acre plots not far from present-day picnic areas along Glover Road. Among the items found on one parcel was the metal figure of an African American man — part of a toy representing a mule cart driver, once a common occupation for black males.

An iron figurine about 3½ inches tall (left) was recovered at the site of Charles Dickson's home. It may have come from a toy mule cart such as the antique collectible above.

Elijah and Sarah Whitby rented property near where Broad Branch flows into Rock Creek, paying Isaac Shoemaker three dollars a month for a two-room house and a stable. Based on pottery found at the site, researchers say the home may have been built in the early 1800s and was probably occupied for decades by African Americans. [See the top of the previous page for an artist's conception of the house, based on 1880s drawings by the Smithsonian's Delancey Gill.] By 1900, Sarah was a widow, raising nine children and working as a laundress. Some evidence of her clientele was found among the 52 buttons unearthed on the property. One was inscribed "Saville Row," the neighborhood that housed London's finest tailors.

Documenting these households represents one way to honor the memory of the many African Americans who made essential contributions to the history of Rock Creek Valley. Acknowledging the injustices they faced helps us appreciate the modern era in which all visitors are welcome to experience together the beauty of Rock Creek Park.

Whitby house re-creation, mule cart driver, typical cart figurine, CWA work crew at Piney Branch Parkway (1930s): National Park Service; Contrabands at Camp Brightwood in 2nd R.I. Camp (1861) and *Celebration of the abolition of slavery in the District of Columbia by the colored people, in Washington, April 19, 1866* (sketched by Frederick Dielman in *Harper's weekly* 5/12/1866): Library of Congress; Peirce slave petition: Emancipation in the District of Columbia (Treasury Secretary report filed with the House of Representatives 1/17/1864).

D is for Dumbarton

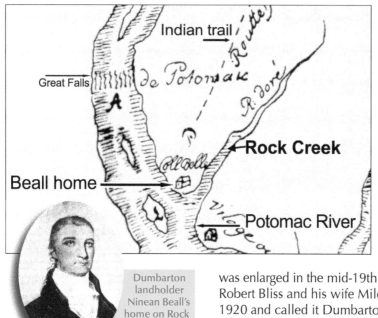

The name Dumbarton has been part of Rock Creek history for more than 300 years, dating back to a plot of land called Rock of Dumbarton.

The word Dumbarton is from the Gaelic *Dun Breatann*, meaning Fortress of the Britons. It describes an actual rock in Scotland, rising in two peaks above the waters where two rivers meet. A castle has guarded that strategic high ground since the 1220s.

A Scottish immigrant named Ninian Beall established his Rock of Dumbarton in 1703 at the point where Rock Creek meets the Potomac River. Beall was remarkable in appearance, longevity and accomplishment. Tall and brawny with long red hair, he had been taken prisoner by the English army in Scotland, served five years as an indentured servant in Barbados and Maryland, and then prospered in the New World — amassing some 25,000 acres of land by the time he died at age 92. He also earned the title of Founder of Georgetown, the city that grew up around his 800-acre Rock of Dumbarton.

Thanks to a 1712 map (left), Beall is the first person documented to have lived along Rock Creek. Another feature on the map is an Indian trail, which more or less became Wisconsin Avenue.

House and Gardens

A house was built in 1801 within the original Rock of Dumbarton parcel on the highest point in Georgetown. The home was enlarged in the mid-19th century and named The Oaks. US diplomat Robert Bliss and his wife Mildred Barnes Bliss purchased the mansion in 1920 and called it Dumbarton Oaks. They not only preserved the house, they hired landscape architect Beatrix Farrand to create one of America's greatest showplaces of landscape design. Farrand, the nation's first

Indian trail

Great Falls

Rock Creek

Beall home

Potomac River

Dumbarton landholder Ninean Beall's home on Rock Creek is shown on this 1712 map.

female professional landscape architect, arranged formal gardens near the mansion, which gave way to informal gardens and finally to a naturalistic setting highlighted by newly created ponds and waterfalls.

For their 30th wedding anniversary, the couple commissioned a chamber piece by Igor Stravinsky. The *Concerto in E-flat*, subtitled *Dumbarton Oaks*, had its private premiere at the estate in 1938, four weeks before its public debut in Paris.

Robert and Mildred Bliss would give us much more than a piece of music. In 1940, they donated the entire property. Mr. Bliss's alma mater, Harvard University, received the mansion (top right) and formal gardens. They have become the Dumbarton Oaks Research Library and Collection, whose gardens and celebrated exhibits of Byzantine, Pre-Columbian and European art are open to the public. The United Nations was formulated in 1944 at a conference at Dumbarton Oaks.

The historic mansion on the Dumbarton Oaks estate now houses a research center and priceless art and book collections.

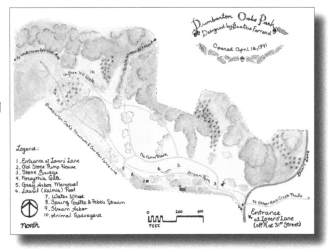

Two of Rock Creek's Sister Parks

The remaining 27 acres became a gift to the American people — Dumbarton Oaks Park (right), now managed by Rock Creek Park and supported by the Dumbar-

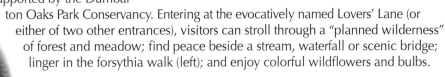

ton Oaks Park Conservancy. Entering at the evocatively named Lovers' Lane (or either of two other entrances), visitors can stroll through a "planned wilderness" of forest and meadow; find peace beside a stream, waterfall or scenic bridge; linger in the forsythia walk (left); and enjoy colorful wildflowers and bulbs.

Next door — also under Rock Creek supervision — is Montrose Park, 16 acres of a parcel originally called Parrott's Woods. During the early 19th century, rope tycoon Robert Parrott would let Georgetown residents visit his property for picnics and other gatherings. His workers used the long walkway lit by gas lamps as a "ropewalk"— the place where rope was braided.

The Other Dumbarton House

A home built in 1799 on another part of the original Rock of Dumbarton tract was renamed Dumbarton House by the National Society of the Colonial Dames of America after the group had it restored with 18th and 19th century furniture and decorative arts. Since 1932 it has served as a museum and the Society's headquarters. Dumbarton House also has a connection with the Dumbarton (or Q Street) Bridge over Rock Creek. The home was moved about 100 feet north in 1915 to allow Q Street to be extended to the bridge and to the Dupont Circle area beyond.

Dumbarton Oaks Park Stone Bridge, 1960s and 1712 map by Swiss explorer Baron Christoph von Graffenreid: National Park Service. Ninian Beall portrait from Sally Somervell Mackall, *Early Days of Washington* (1899). Dumbarton Oaks mansion and Dumbarton Oaks Park Forsythia Walk: (Jack E. Boucher), Historic American Buildings Survey, Library of Congress. Map of Dumbarton Oaks Park by Sophia McCrocklin, used by permission of the artist and Dumbarton Oaks Park Conservancy.

E is for Ecology

It's tough maintaining an urban park.

Beyond the forests, meadows and streams of Rock Creek Valley, the city continually intrudes on the Park's ecology — its web of life in which countless species of plants and animals interact with each other and with their environment.

Because of the air pollution of a large metropolitan area, acid rain poisons the streams and high summer ozone levels stress trees and plants.

Rock Creek Park was designed to be a wilderness in the city. That is a challenging ecology to protect.

Dense development paves over the places where water can soak into the soil. Rainfall then carries pollutants like road salt and fertilizer into the creeks.

Sometimes pollutants come from human activity — as in the 1990 leak of 8,000 gallons of heating oil behind a Connecticut Avenue condominium and the massive fish kill in 2000 when an exterminating company employee washed pesticides down a storm drain.

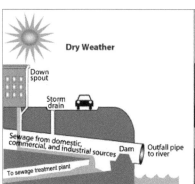
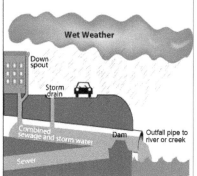
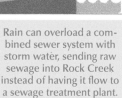

Rain can overload a combined sewer system with storm water, sending raw sewage into Rock Creek instead of having it flow to a sewage treatment plant.

Geysers of Sewage

A long-outdated sanitation system lets raw sewage seep into the creek beds. Most dramatically, several manholes erupted in geysers of sewage in June 1952 when the main trunk line parallel to Rock Creek became overloaded by sewage from DC and Montgomery County. One site dubbed "Old Faithful" spewed sewage at a rate of 20 gallons per second.

Less spectacular spills happen after any hard rain because parts of the DC sanitation system combine sewage and stormwater in the same pipe. Whenever stormwater inundates the system, raw sewage is dumped into local waterways. These overflows happen about 30 times a year into Rock Creek and 75 times annually into the Anacostia and Potomac rivers.

Unusually heavy downpours also overwhelm water habitats, flood buildings, undermine roads and trails, and wash away bridges, trees and picnic tables.

Invaded by Pests, Plants and Bambi

Non-native vegetation is crowding out local species. Though English ivy aggressively chokes trees and ground cover, it has long been a popular landscaping plant — introduced by both homeowners and the planners who designed Meridian Hill and Montrose Parks. Japanese honeysuckle was a significant part of the Olmsted Brothers' 1918 plan for Rock Creek Park — yet it outcompetes nearly all native foliage in its path. These and other pernicious plants — including porcelainberry, mock strawberry, garlic mustard and celandine — also get a foothold when seeds are transported by birds or the wind and when landscaping waste is dumped in or near the Park.

Other invaders include non-native insects — gypsy moths, emerald ash borers, and an aphid-like bug that destroys hemlocks and firs — and various fungi that cause chestnut blight and Dutch elm disease and attack flowering dogwoods.

The area is also being overrun by white-tailed deer. They damage existing plants, eat tree seedlings so that the forest can no longer regenerate and take food and cover away from other wildlife. A 2009 natural resource assessment called the overabundance of deer the Park's "largest internal threat." The National Park Service established an initial goal of reducing the deer population to 15 to 20 per square mile — down from the 82 per square mile estimated by sampling in 2007.

Meanwhile, climate change promotes weather extremes and upsets the age-old calendar of the seasons.

Above, white-tailed buck. Left, from top: invasive porcelainberry, gypsy moth, orange bark cankers of chestnut blight.

Preserving Our Park

These challenges are being taken seriously. Rock Creek Park has a management plan to try to control the deer population. Groups such as Rock Creek Conservancy and Dumbarton Oaks Conservancy recruit "weed warriors" to root out invasive vegetation. Horticulturalists fight insects and disease with biological and chemical controls, pest barriers and new plantings of resistant species. Area gardeners are favoring native plants.

Within the Rock Creek watershed, neighborhoods are marking storm drains with reminders that anything going down the drain can flow into the creek. Households are taking advantage of programs and grants to plant trees and to reduce stormwater runoff by installing rain barrels, rain gardens and permeable walkways and driveways. In two sites off Oregon Avenue and one adjoining Broad Branch, the District has built a series of pools descending in steps to slow the flow of stormwater runoff and filter out impurities before they reach the streams.

Finally, the DC Water and Sewer Authority is working to prevent the overflow of sewage into creeks and rivers whenever there's a significant rain. Giant machines have bored enormous underground tunnels to serve as holding tanks for sewage and stormwater until the rain can subside. One such tunnel had been slated for Piney Branch — but was scrapped in favor of new green infrastructure in neighborhoods near Rock Creek aimed at capturing rainwater before it washes into the sewer system.

It will take the collective effort of residents and governments, volunteers and organizations to preserve the oldest urban park in the National Park System as a natural oasis within the Nation's Capital.

A Rock Creek Conservancy volunteer cuts woody stems of English ivy, an invasive vine that chokes out native vegetation, deprives leaves of sunlight, promotes disease and grows heavy enough to topple trees.

Carolina wren: Matthew Sileo/MatthewSileoPhotography.com; flower, fish: adapted from Springbeauty, Spotfin shiner, Brian Gratwicke, DCNature.com under Creative Commons 2.5 license; landscape: Lorraine Swerdloff; porcelainberry, gypsy moth, chestnut blight: National Park Service; buck: David Swerdloff; RCC volunteer: Margo Reid; sanitation diagram: EPA.

F is for Fords

Splashing through Rock Creek used to be both a delight and a danger for area drivers.

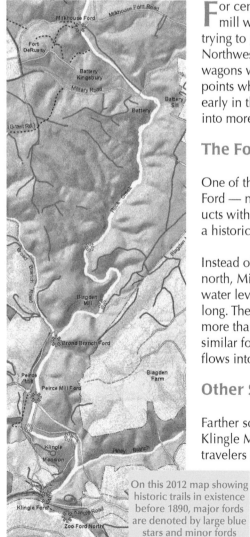

For centuries, a stream powerful enough to turn mill wheels also created a barrier for travelers trying to go east and west through what is now Northwest Washington. When farmers filled their wagons with crops and millers loaded grain for market, they looked for the points where Rock Creek was shallowest. There they forded the stream — and, early in the history of Rock Creek Park, some of these locations were improved into more formal fords.

The Ford at the Milkhouse

One of the oldest crossings is the only one that has been preserved. Milkhouse Ford — named after an actual milkhouse on Rock Creek that chilled dairy products with the stream's cool water — was originally part of Milkhouse Ford Road, a historic east-west route replaced during the Civil War by nearby Military Road.

Instead of building a bridge across Rock Creek as Beach Drive was extended north, Milkhouse Ford was paved in 1904. Concrete was laid below the normal water level of the creek some six to eight inches thick, 24 feet wide and 74 feet long. The goal was to provide a solid surface where the creek would flow no more than three inches deep most of the year. You can still see remnants of a similar ford constructed at the foot of Blagden Avenue, near where Broad Branch flows into Rock Creek.

Other Splash-throughs

Farther south was Klingle Ford, whose historic name is shared today with the Klingle Mansion, built in 1823, and Klingle Road, laid out in 1831. While travelers along Rock Creek had to depend on the ford, Klingle Road had its own bridge, referenced in the first sentence of the 1890 law that authorized Rock Creek Park as "beginning at Klingle Ford Bridge, and running northwardly."

On this 2012 map showing historic trails in existence before 1890, major fords are denoted by large blue stars and minor fords by small stars.

Two other fords, one just above and the other just below the National Zoo, required travelers on Beach Drive to forge through the water.

Many people alive today recall with some glee driving to the zoo or even commuting through some of Rock Creek's fords. But, as the *Evening Star* wrote in 1956 about the zoo fords, "the slightest flash rain usually is enough to force zoo police to haul out the ford barriers and route disgruntled motorists back to city streets." The *Star* noted that both zoo fords had been closed all day for 122 days of the previous year and closed part of the day on 62 other occasions.

Narrow Escapes

Any ford can be dangerous. In June 1908, President Theodore Roosevelt was riding a skittish horse that had second thoughts about crossing Broad Branch Ford. It reared and fell, throwing both Teddy and his mount into the stream. As the *Washington Post* reported, "the President's fall … took him completely clear of the horse, and to that circumstance he probably owes his life."

A flooded ford was especially treacherous. Also in 1908 at the same location, high water swept an automobile into the surging creek. According to the *Post*, two occupants jumped into the water, and "standing waist deep … rescued their wives, carrying them to shore in their arms." After heavy thunderstorms in 1939, a car stalled on Klingle Ford. The *Evening Star* noted that just before the vehicle went careening "downstream like a wood box," the driver "picked up his dog Mickey and waded ashore."

Lingering into the Recent Past

One by one, the fords were replaced. A bridge built in 1926 allowed drivers to bypass Milkhouse Ford — though a wet crossing remained an option until 1994. Today you can look, but not cross.

Cars in the 1920s using Broad Branch Ford to cross Rock Creek just south of where the two streams intersect. The bridge in the background spanned Broad Branch.

The Porter Street bridge replaced Klingle Ford in 1947. The intersection of Broach Branch Road and Beach Drive was re-engineered in the mid-1950s, replacing both Broad Branch Ford and the adjacent Pebble Dash Bridge. Finally, it took the completion of the zoo tunnel in 1966 for travelers on Beach Drive to forgo the zoo fords.

Proposals to build the zoo tunnel had accelerated with the opening of the Rock Creek and Potomac Parkway in 1936. But the Parkway also inspired controversial plans to extend the highway north along the creek. Before a tunnel could be built, the question that had to be answered was: what kind of road would the tunnel lead to? For three decades it was unclear whether it would continue as a shady, two-lane road — or transform into a four-lane expressway connecting with Klingle Road or Colorado Avenue or perhaps continuing north along Oregon Avenue into Maryland as far as East-West Highway or even to the future I-270.

A final answer was elusive because all parties had to agree: the District, the National Park Service and (since the route went through the zoo) the Smithsonian — with the National Capital Park and Planning Commission and Maryland authorities also weighing in. This stalemate prevented the construction of an expressway until attention turned instead to building the Beltway and Metro. Thus Beach Drive stayed a sylvan two-lane road and the fords remained open well into the 1960s as a vestige of Rock Creek history.

Volkswagen in Milkhouse Ford (9/26/1965) and Historic trail map (2012): National Park Service; ford near Broad Branch (1920s): Washingtoniana Collection, DC Public Library; news articles (clockwise from upper left): *Washington Post* 5/8/1908, 6/4/1908, 9/30/1902, *Evening Star* 4/1/1912.

CAB STRANDS AT FORD

Party in Automobile Caught in Swift Current.

MEN CARRY WOMEN TO SHORE

SHIES WHILE FORDING STREAM

Frightened Horse Puts Occupants of Carriage in Danger.

Henry Hunt McKee, cashier of the National Capital Bank, and Mrs. McKee had an exciting experience yesterday afternoon while driving over the Blagden avenue ford in Rock Creek Park. They were seated in a buggy, and when the horse was almost across the creek it became frightened...

Mr. Roosevelt Put in Peril of Life By Horse.

THROWN AT ROCK CREEK PARK

Steed Falls on Its Back in Water Beside Executive, Who Clears Saddle as Animal Rears—Rider, Bruised by Rocks, Has Narrow Escape From Hoofs of Mount.

CAUGHT BY RUSHING WATER

Lieut. Commander Hayden's Narrow Escape from Rock Creek.

Attempted to Ford When Stream Was Swollen and Carriage Upset—Lost His Crutches in the Water.

Lieut. Commander E. E. Hayden, of the United States navy, had a narrow escape from death last Friday, and but for the prudence...

G is for Geology

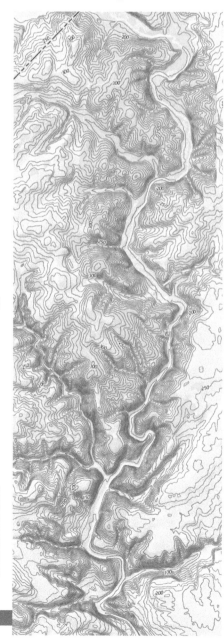

Where did the rocks in
Rock Creek come from?

The huge boulders and large outcrops of granite and other bedrock within Rock Creek Park were once part of mountains formed when volcanic islands slammed into the North American coastline about 450 million years ago. Over time, the mountains eroded, leaving behind the rolling hills of the Piedmont.

Through heat, pressure and faulting within the rock, the stone itself fractured and deformed. Today some of the exposed rock still reveals the effects of these geologic processes in kinks and folds, in veins of quartz and other minerals that filled in the spaces, in reddish-brown dots of embedded garnet, and at sites where blocks of rock are offset along faults.

The action of rain, gravity and flowing water, along with repeated freezing and thawing, began weathering the rock at its weakest points along cracks and folds. Some of the rock was more resistant to erosion, making it impossible for the streams to carve out broad, flat channels. Instead, the Park's creek beds twist and turn.

Plains, Rapids and Terraces

Just east of the Park, the Piedmont meets the younger and flatter Coastal Plain, made up of sandstone and other sedimentary rock deposited less than 100 million years ago and prone to more uniform erosion. At the boundary where the two formations intersect, waterways spill out from the Piedmont in rapids and waterfalls.

The geology of Washington illustrates continuous shifts over time. Over the past few million years, periodic drops in sea levels and local uplifts caused the streams and rivers to cut deeper channels into the landscape, eroding ancient bedrock. With each round of change, the previous flat river

A contour map of Rock Creek Park (shown here from Klingle Valley to the District line) reveals the landscape's twisting creek beds and forested terraces.

bottom was left high and dry. The result was a series of broad terraces across the city, rising like steps from the Potomac. One place to appreciate these plateaus is Meridian Hill Park, which is bordered north and south by terraces that today give a fine view of old DC.

The intersection of the Piedmont and Coastal Plain coincides with a large system of faults running down the center of the Park, called the Rock Creek Shear Zone. The wildest parts of Rock Creek — between Boulder Bridge and Military Road — show ample evidence of the Shear Zone and the transition from Piedmont to Plain, as whitewater splashes among countless boulders severed and smoothed from the remains of ancient mountains.

(Geo-)Logical Conclusions

Geology has created opportunity. Colonial settlers took advantage of the rushing water by erecting mills along the banks of Rock Creek. Water percolating through terraces and coursing through fissures formed springs that were once an important part of the Washington water supply. Some of the rock outcrops were utilized by ancient Native Americans who shaped quartzite stones into tools and spearheads and worked soapstone into cooking pots.

Over the past two centuries, newer quarry sites provided the familiar "Rock Creek granite" (technically, Kensington Tonalite) used for structures, chimneys, walls and bridges within the Park. At least 17 quarries were in operation in the Rock Creek Park area barely a century ago — and we can visit what remains of some of them along Broad Branch, above the Melvin Hazen tributary and just upstream from Montrose Park.

The proximity of Piedmont and Coastal Plain has given Rock Creek Park a rich diversity in minerals and rock in a relatively small area. It also helps explain some of the variety of plant life, with coastal vegetation coexisting with more mountain-loving plants.

Only occasionally can we observe Rock Creek flowing with the power that once turned mill wheels. Springs and entire tributaries of the creek have disappeared or declined — some of them paved over or replaced by drainage and sewer pipes. Piney Branch, for example, was once an extensive water system in its own right. Today its natural course upstream ends at 16th Street — though its former path is traced northeast by Arkansas Avenue. One sign of progress is the "daylighting" of a 1,600-foot section of Broad Branch that had been diverted into a pipe during the 1930s. In 2014, the stream was brought back into the open air, restoring a natural part of the geology of Rock Creek Park.

G is for Glover

G also is for Glover

As a boy, Charles Carroll Glover (1846-1936) rambled around the wooded hills of Washington. The story goes that he was part of a group of lads trying to steal cherries from the orchards near Peirce Mill when Joshua Peirce stormed out of his mansion toting a shotgun. Peirce caught young Charles, who apologized and offered to pay for the fruit — and the two became friends.

Charles Glover not only was instrumental in creating Rock Creek Park, his name is on another park that helped launch America's environmental movement.

The RIGGS NATIONAL BANK OF WASHINGTON D.C.

Charles Glover outside the headquarters of Riggs National Bank in 1915. A 1922 newspaper ad (above) promotes its location "on Pennsylvania Avenue facing the US Treasury."

Glover grew up to become Washington's leading banker, although he began at Riggs and Company as a lowly clerk. Among his many philanthropic efforts, he led the final push for the creation of Rock Creek Park — on land that included the Peirce property. To build support, he led a group of influential Washingtonians on a ride through Rock Creek Valley on Thanksgiving Day 1888, and then hosted a strategy session at his home a few days later.

The citizens committee formed to push for the park included other prominent bankers and landowners. Brainard Warner had his own real estate firm and was president of both Columbia National Bank and Washington Loan and Trust. Alexander Britton was second in command at Columbia National and president of American Security and Trust. Other members were in a position to sway public opinion: *Evening Star* editor Crosby Noyes, *Baltimore Sun* correspondent Frank Richardson, and *National Tribune* founder and real estate mogul George Lemon.

Convincing Congress

Rock Creek Park opponents assailed Glover and his moneyed allies as promoting the legislation only to increase the value of their own investments. New York representative Francis Spinola told Congress, "the gentlemen who own this land are shrewd, cunning real estate operators" and he intended "to protect the treasury of the country against … such invasions as this bill proposes." Critics recalled the unchecked spending by Alexander "Boss" Shepherd that had left DC bankrupt in 1874 — and they opposed new appropriations, especially for a park that would only benefit Washingtonians.

The committee — aided by active lobbying by Glover — succeeded in crafting a compromise lawmakers could support. Half the cost of Rock Creek Park would be paid by the District, and the federal government would get the benefit of any new assessments on nearby property owners if the park increased the value of their land. The Rock Creek Park bill was signed into law on September 27, 1890 — less than two years after the committee first met.

Success did not keep Glover from pressing for additional parkland within the District. Nor did it keep lawmakers from questioning his motives. In 1913, Tennessee Congressman Thetus Sims accused Glover of trying to "unload" property on the federal government at inflated prices. The Speaker of the House had to reprimand Glover for his response, which was to assault Sims in Farragut Square.

SIMS TELLS OF ATTACK AS GLOVER APOLOGIZES TO HOUSE INQUISITORS

Congressman Declares He Thought Financier Insane When Pair Met in Park—Feared Shooting—Witnesses Describe Combat. One Saw Fray From Treetop.

BANKER SORRY LAW BARS DUELING, BEN JOHNSON INFORMS COMMITTEE

Glover's Letter to Committee Head

News coverage of Glover's 1913 encounter with Congressman Thetus Sims included the banker's letter of apology and allegations Glover "regretted … he could not challenge Mr. Sims to a duel."

Glover led the effort to fill in the marshy Potomac Flats, which became the home of the Jefferson and Lincoln Memorials. Outside of government, he bankrolled the initial costs for the National Cathedral, served as president of the Corcoran Gallery of Art, and helped develop his own neighborhood along Massachusetts Avenue, which evolved into Embassy Row.

Glover's name has been memorialized by Glover Road within Rock Creek Park, Glover Bridge taking Massachusetts Avenue over Rock Creek, and the Glover Park neighborhood. But his name is also part of the title of another park in the Rock Creek system.

Tale of Two Benefactors

Glover Archbold Park began with nearly 80 acres of wooded land donated by Glover in 1923 in the valley of the Foundry Branch creek. The next year, Washington socialite and world explorer Anne Archbold (1873-1968) added another 28 acres from her holdings in Georgetown. The daughter of oil tycoon John Dustin Archbold, she had established the estate known as Hillandale off Reservoir Road. Frequent guests included Eleanor Roosevelt, Queen Elizabeth, Noel Coward and Leopold Stokowski. Archbold also used the grounds to raise sheep and train seeing-eye and police dogs.

Archbold's main house was a country villa in the Italian Renaissance style, finished in 1925 but in disrepair by 1990 (right). The part of the estate not donated as parkland now houses the Hillandale development and the French chancery.

The tracts they donated formed a long ribbon of green originally called Glover Archbold Parkway and initially designed to be the site of a scenic highway. The District didn't make any moves to build the road until after World War II. By then, it was clear such a parkway would be used as a commuter route instead of being the quiet country road originally imagined. Archbold rose in opposition, proposing instead that "the beautiful wooded valley be preserved perpetually … and be enjoyed by all as a natural sanctuary." In 1967, a little more than a year before she died, DC authorities gave up the right-of-way through the park.

During the battle over the parkway, a writer and editor for the US Fish and Wildlife Service often visited Glover Archbold Park to observe nature and study the environment. Her name was Rachel Carson (right), and her 1962 book *Silent Spring* became a major inspiration for the American environmental movement. In 2013 Congress designated the Glover Archbold Park hiking path — which might have become a highway — as the Rachel Carson Nature Trail.

The main trail in Glover Archbold Park (left) extends more than three miles along the route of Foundry Branch creek from Van Ness Street to the C&O Canal. Many visitors create longer loop hikes and runs— connecting with the trail up Rock Creek by taking advantage of the canal towpath and paths through Melvin C. Hazen, Whitehaven and Dumbarton Oaks Parks.

Glover photos (c.1905, 1915): Library of Congress; Riggs ad: *Washington Post* 3/15/1922; Sims article: *Washington Times* 4/22/1913; Archbold article: *Evening Star* 10/23/1924 reprinted with permission of the DC Public Library, *Star* Collection ©*Washington Post*; Hillandale photo (Kim Prothro Williams 1990), map: National Park Service; Park photos: David and Lorraine Swerdloff; Carson photo: US Fish & Wildlife Service.

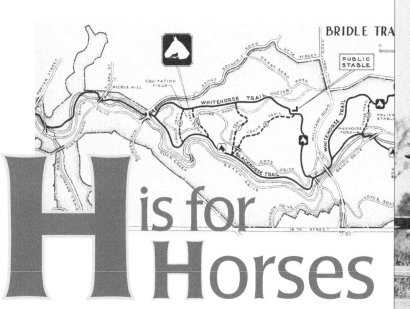

Some Horse Center workers still refer to the "White Horse" and "Black Horse" trails that appear on this 1958 Park map.

When Theodore Roosevelt died, the *Washington Times* put the photo at left on the front page, calling it "the most famous picture of Theodore Roosevelt, specially posed and taken in Rock Creek Park."

H is for Horses

Rock Creek Park has always been a place for horses. The 1890 authorization act required construction of bridle paths "as soon as practicable."

Most rides along the Park's 13 miles of equestrian trails begin at the Rock Creek Park Horse Center. A mural that fills the office wall shows five of the most loved horses ever to have lived at the Center — Jackson, Buster, Hopi, Bennie Fluff and Papa Snoogums. Each one taught a generation of children how to ride.

The Center offers private and group lessons for all ages, mainly in English riding, lower-level jumping and dressage. You can join in regularly scheduled, supervised rides along Park trails. Other programs include pony rides for kids and riding camps for youngsters, teens and adults. Of the dozens of horses at the Center, about half are "schoolies" for classes and trail rides. The rest are boarded at the stables.

Therapeutic riding instructors have worked at the Center since 1974, helping clients ranging from students with emotional, developmental and physical disabilities to America's wounded warriors. Nancy Reagan was a prominent supporter of the program that would go on to benefit White House Press Secretary James Brady after he was wounded in the assassination attempt on President Reagan in 1981.

Hoofbeats from the Past

Horses have been a familiar sight in Rock Creek Valley for centuries. Not only did they provide basic transportation, many were the literal workhorses of the area's farmers and millers. Others were part of cavalry units that clashed near the creek during the Civil War. But Washingtonians also learned early on that a ride along the few country roads into the valley made for a pleasant respite from city life.

You didn't even need your own horse. By 1863 you could take a stagecoach from downtown for 75 cents roundtrip to two destinations overlooking Rock Creek. The Crystal Springs resort was located near where the tennis stadium is today. Just to the north was a destination all about horses. The Piney Branch Trotting Course (later, Brightwood Driving Park) attracted harness racing fans beginning in the 1840s or 50s until the track closed in 1909.

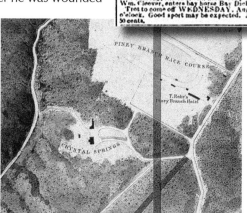

An 1867 map shows both the Piney Branch Trotting Course and Crystal Springs resort. Rock Creek is the curved line at left. Added shading denotes the approximate location of present-day 16th Street and Colorado Avenue. 16th Street was extended north over Piney Branch and through the oval track in 1909, ending six decades of racing.
Inset: *Evening Star* advertisement from 1860.

Beach Drive and other early routes constructed within the Park were originally carriage roads. They opened the valley to scenic visits by horse and buggy before automobiles became popular. Equestrian paths were quickly established, often tracing the routes of historic trails. An "electric eye" was installed on one bridle path in 1922 to give traffic on Tilden Street a red light so that horses could cross.

Hunts and Horse Shows

In the early decades of the Park, horsemen and women used the area for fox hunts, often gathering at Peirce Mill. The American tradition was to chase, but not kill, the fox — and sometimes these "hunts" focused more on riding and jumping than following a scent.

Horse and rider compete at the Equitation Field, October 1967.

After the Brightwood Reservoir opened in 1900 on the west side of 16th Street above Colorado Avenue, parkland cleared alongside became the site of frequent horse shows up until World War II. Horse exhibitions have also been held at the Park's Equitation Field on Ridge Road since the late 1930s. Equitation relates to a rider's posture and control — and the name Equitation Field hearkens back to old social gatherings of horse lovers. Today's Equitation Field remains a place for people to meet and exercise their horses.

A horsewoman encounters a car on Milkhouse Ford around 1960.

History as Horse Opera

The curious chronology of the Horse Center begins in 1957 with the announcement that the National Park Service would not only build the first stable in the Park, it would build two of them. One for the upper valley opened in late 1958 near Glover Road, but only after plans to put the facility next to a Park Police stable on Oregon Avenue were scuttled by neighbors and by gardeners who would lose their plots.

The stable in the lower valley was operated by the man behind Edgewater Riding Academy, which had lost its site to construction of the Theodore Roosevelt Bridge. The new Edgewater Academy opened in 1959 in the shadow of the Taft Bridge. Building of the Metro's Red Line forced it to close in 1970.

In response, transit officials erected a replacement near the site of the then-bankrupt Glover Road stable. The Rock Creek Park Horse Center opened in 1972 with 57 horse stalls, two outdoor rings and one indoor ring. Park Police went on to use the Edgewater property for their new stable which today also provides training for mounted units from the Army, Secret Service, Capitol Police and police departments around the country.

The horse trails through Rock Creek Valley continue to offer a convenient escape into wilderness. From the saddle, riders gain a point of view and a connection to the natural world that would have been familiar to Washingtonians many generations ago.

1958 Bridle Trail map, Fall Horse Show (1967), Milkhouse Ford (circa 1960): National Park Service; *Theodore Roosevelt on horseback jumping over a split rail fence* (1902), portion of *Topographical sketch of the environs of Washington, D.C.* (N. Michler, 1867): Library of Congress; *Evening Star* ad: 7/31/1860; scene at Horse Center: David Swerdloff.

Classes at the Rock Creek Park Horse Center teach riding skills.

I is for American Indians

1590 engraving of a Native chief in Virginia

Although ancient Native Americans did not establish settlements up Rock Creek, they were frequent visitors.

It was probably 13,000 years ago, as glaciers advanced as far south as Pennsylvania, that indigenous people first came to Rock Creek Valley. They were nomadic hunter-gatherers living on berries, nuts and roots, along with game ranging from beavers to mastodons. Fast-forward several millennia, and a warmer climate melted the glaciers — creating rivers, streams and the Chesapeake Bay. Though larger animals died out, a rich variety of fish and plant life allowed the Indians to form more permanent villages, perhaps even at the mouth of Rock Creek.

About 4,000 years ago, these Native Americans left behind the first evidence of visits to the valley. In addition to using the area as hunting and fishing grounds, they also had journeyed from their riverside villages to take advantage of Rock Creek's rocks.

Dark shading in 1897 map denotes Indian quarry sites in hillsides between the DC neighborhoods of Crestwood (top) and Mount Pleasant (bottom). Added shading shows Piney Branch creek (blue) and the route of present-day 16th Street (green).

Camping and Quarrying

Archeological evidence shows that Indians established campgrounds in the bluffs above Rock Creek. Most prominently in the hillsides overlooking Piney Branch, they pried away stones of quartzite using deer antlers, bone tools or wooden levers. They broke the stones into almond-shaped forms several inches long, which they took back to camp and shaped into spear points. Natives also carved cooking vessels from boulders of soapstone they quarried in the area we today call Soapstone Valley.

One of America's first renowned archeologists, William Henry Holmes of the Smithsonian's Bureau of American Ethnology, studied these quarry and camp sites between 1889 and 1894. He realized that the countless chunks of quartzite left behind represented stone that had been rejected and discarded.

Further Digging

Other archeologically significant sites along Rock Creek have been discovered in the shadow of the Whitehurst Freeway. The wide variety of arrowheads, spear points and pottery pieces suggest that these places were used as camping grounds by Native peoples time and again from some 6,000 years ago until the arrival of Europeans.

Quartzite rock, as it would have been shaped from oval "blank" to finished spear point.

In one pit about 250 feet east of Rock Creek, archeologists unearthed the remains of a woman who had been cremated and then buried along with such artifacts as shark teeth, a comb carved from an antler and woven cloth made of pawpaw fiber. Because these objects are similar to those found in Native American graves in New York and Delaware, researchers believe the "Whitehurst Woman" could represent the first wave of Algonquians into the Chesapeake region about 1,300 years ago. Around this time, indians were establishing a network of foot trails that served as trade routes along the East Coast and as far inland as the Ohio Valley.

Discovered in the same pit as the buried remains of the "Whitehurst Woman" were fragments of a comb made from antler.

Colonial History

In 1608 Captain John Smith sailed up the Potomac, and his party may have been the first non-Indians to observe Rock Creek. The Natives encountered by Smith and other early European explorers lived in sizable towns during the spring and fall when they planted and harvested corn. In other seasons, groups of Natives would go on hunting and fishing expeditions — and Rock Creek Valley was a likely destination.

The arrival of Europeans scattered the local Algonquian Indians — including tribes whose names may sound familiar today, including the Patawomeck, Patuxant, Piscataway, Mattawomen and various tribes controlled by Powhatan. New diseases decimated their populations. The Susquehannock, Massawomeck and other tribes sent war parties into the area, vying for dominance. France and England also used allies among the Indians to attack their enemies. The violence made Rock Creek Valley too dangerous for new settlers. Only when the 1722 Treaty of Albany provided some peace and stability did tenant farmers — many of them new German and Scottish immigrants — move into the wilderness and establish the first farms in the area that is now Rock Creek Park.

Even well into the 18th century, colonists used as landmarks so-called "Indian old fields" — including one clearing near the confluence of Broad Branch and Rock Creek. In these places, Native Americans may have burned away sections of forest to generate new growth that would attract game.

This section of a 1624 map based on the early explorations of John Smith shows Indian tribes, towns and place names along the Potomac River. North is to the right — with the approximate location of the future District of Columbia (and Rock Creek) denoted by a green star. Across the river (near the present-day Pentagon) was a Native settlement called Namoraughquend, which Smith was told meant "place where fish are caught."

Indians and the Park

Rock Creek Park includes the Indian quarry sites along Piney Branch thanks to lobbying during the 1920s by William Henry Holmes himself. He called the land "a sacred spot" which deserved preservation "not only on account of its romantic beauty" but also because it was "the site on which for hundreds, possibly thousands of years, the Indian tribes of the Potomac Valley quarried quartzite boulders from which they roughed out … their implements of war and the chase."

Klingle Mansion also has an Indian connection. After Joshua Peirce Klingle inherited the property from uncle Joshua Peirce in 1869, Mrs. Klingle hung two portraits in the parlor depicting her ancestors: Pocahontas and Powhatan. Some of the same Native American tribes described by John Smith live on today — and several have succeeded in their hard-won effort to gain official recognition. Many local families still trace their ancestry to American Indians who settled along the Potomac.

Chieftain of Virginia (engraving by Theodor de Bry after watercolor by John White), 1590: Library of Congress; quarry map: *Fifteenth annual report of the Bureau of Ethnography to the Secretary of the Smithsonian Institution*, 1893-94 (1897); Quartzite progression from blank to spear point, Whitehurst comb: National Park Service; *Virginia, discovered and discribed by Captayn John Smith, 1606; graven by William Hole* (London, 1624): Library of Congress.

J is for the Joaquin Miller Cabin

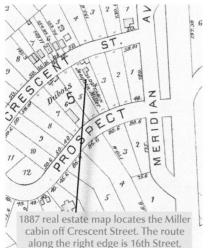

Joaquin Miller sits in a rocking chair in front of his cabin in its original location on Meridian Hill.

Though he became a famous poet and playwright, Joaquin Miller's most original creation may have been the image he crafted of himself. Born Cincinnatus Heine Miller, he took on the name Joaquin *(hwa-'keen)* after a Mexican bandit and fashioned himself into the quintessential frontiersman.

Who was Joaquin Miller and what is his log cabin doing in the middle of Rock Creek Park?

His writings drew on his many adventures in the West. He experienced the California Gold Rush, lived for a year in a Native American village and worked at jobs that ranged from newspaper editor, lawyer and judge to Pony Express rider, mining camp cook and horse thief. His writings became so celebrated in the United States and Britain, he was hailed as the "Poet of the Sierras" and the "Byron of the Rockies." Nearly every American schoolchild could recite his poem "Columbus," which ended, "He gained a world; he gave that world / Its greatest lesson: 'On! sail on!'"

1887 real estate map locates the Miller cabin off Crescent Street. The route along the right edge is 16th Street, which had been extended north from Boundary Street (Florida Avenue) to replace Meridian Avenue. Prospect is now called Belmont Street.

The Poet Comes to Washington

For more than two years beginning in 1883, Miller was a fixture in Washington, DC — living and working in a two-room log cabin he built on a wooded section of Meridian Hill, just west of 16th Street near present-day Crescent Street. Miller constructed the home from timber cut from what would become Rock Creek Park. For the foundation, President Arthur offered discarded building stone left over from the construction of the Washington Monument. The poet hung animal hides on the walls, put a bearskin on the floor and greeted visitors with a coonskin cap on his head.

At the start, the location on Meridian Hill suited him. According to the *Evening Star*, "(He) tramped for hours at a time over the hills that skirt the city. He declared that he had visited the famous hills of Rome, that he had traveled over France and viewed the busy life of the city from many hilltops, but it was not until he stood on Meridian Hill, where the memories of the colonial and early life of the republic came surging into the observer's mind, that he realized the real charm of a landscape view."

The February 18, 1913 article went on to recount how his notoriety soon attracted too much attention: "Crowds began to flock to the hilltop and seek admission and interviews with the poet…. Soon there was a fence of rustic yet significant character built around the lots, and the cabin door was shut and bolted against all but those whom he knew."

Miller would walk down into the city each day to keep up with political news. He was quoted as saying, "I sit up here in my fine cabin, while the President himself sits down there at the end of the street with his little cabinet."

After Miller left DC in early 1886, the cabin was occupied by new tenants. A 1902 classified reads, "For rent — The Joaquin Miller Cabin; suitable for two or three; high, well-shaded grounds … rent low." When former Ambassador to France Henry White began building a grand house on the property in 1910, White announced that the cabin would have to go.

Cabin at the Creek, (re-)Assembly Required

The California State Association proposed disassembling the structure and re-erecting it in Rock Creek Park as a tribute to Miller, who had settled outside San Francisco. Despite pushback from park authorities, the DC Commissioners approved the plan — as long as the Association picked up all the costs, ceded all control over the cabin and let the engineer in charge of the park choose the exact location (which had to be "on Beach drive north of Military road").

And that is where the Joaquin Miller Cabin came to be rebuilt and still resides. Miller composed a poem (right) to be recited at its dedication on June 2, 1912, about eight months before he died.

The family retained a connection to the cabin. The poet's niece, Pherne Miller, leased the space from 1931 into the 1950s, teaching art and selling refreshments.

Beginning in 1976, an annual program of poetry readings at the cabin celebrated Miller's legacy. The Joaquin Miller Poetry Series moved to the Rock Creek Park Nature Center in 2011.

To My Log Cabin Lovers

Dear, loyal lovers, neighbors mine
 Of California, Washington,
What word of mine, or deed or sign
 Can compensate what ye have done—
This housing in your hearts my home,
 My lowly old Log Cabin home.
Aye, dear the friends and memories
 Of London, Dresden, storied Rome,
The Arctic, the Antipodes,
 But dearer far than all of these
Your holding of my hearth and home—
 My lordly, kingly, Cabin home.
Yea, many hands have been most fair;
 Yea, many trumps of fame and faith
Mine ears have heard both here and there
 That said as only true love saith,
But nothing ever seemed so dear
 As this your brave Log Cabin cheer.

K
is for
Kids

Along with the native plants and animals, our children also thrive in the Park's wild and wooded setting.

Look at Rock Creek Park through young eyes. You see a wilderness inviting you to clamber over boulders, balance on fallen tree trunks, search for fish darting through sunlit patches of water and drop twigs into the creek so you can watch them race downstream.

Each twist in the valley offers a fresh discovery. Every visit provides a different perspective. New encounters offer opportunities to try on new roles.

Science, History, Sports

Budding scientists observe the creatures living in the woods and the lichen growing on trees. They watch the stars at outdoor programs and inside at the only planetarium in the National Park system. They catalog the birds that migrate with the seasons and the others living in the Park year-round.

In Rock Creek and its associated parks, young historians can watch a 19th century mill grind grain, walk Civil War fortifications that saved the Nation's Capital, live like colonial Georgetowners at the Old Stone House and identify the statues on Meridian Hill. And any boy or girl can be a sports hero, thanks to a major league list of activities on ball fields, tennis courts, a golf course, bicycle paths, horse trails and on the water at the Thompson Boat Center.

Where To Begin?

Parents can rely on Park programs and exhibits to help advance the natural curiosity of their youngsters. Families often start at the Rock Creek Park Nature Center. That's Nature Center, not Visitors Center. Even though visitors can get all the maps, brochures and information they need, the name emphasizes that here is a place where children from a very young age can begin a lifelong appreciation of nature. Inside they encounter live animals and exhibits portraying local species. The Discovery Room offers books, puppets, games and other educational activities with an environmental theme for kids as young as pre-K.

At Rock Creek Park Day in 1964, scouts spell out three ways for kids to enjoy the Park.

K is for Kids

Two short self-guided tours begin just outside on the Woodland and Edge of the Woods Trails. From there, kids can stretch their legs and imaginations along many more leafy paths up and down the valley. The other parks under the Rock Creek banner offer their own outdoor experiences — from Potomac River views in Georgetown Waterfront Park to the hedge maze in Montrose Park. Rock Creek's neighbor, the National Zoo, lets youngsters appreciate and help conserve the world's endangered species.

Rangers – Junior and Senior

Park rangers and other staff provide greater depth by leading classes, talks and walks — and by organizing summer camps for students of all ages around such themes as Astronomy and Art in the Park. The TRACK Trail north of Porter Street turns a short hike into an educational treasure hunt. Specialized curricula help educators use park resources to teach key concepts about ecology, science and history.

Volunteer opportunities give youngsters a chance at hands-on experience preserving the environment. And children can aspire to become Junior Rangers, with special activity booklets for ages 6 to 12.

Tent Poles and Swimming Holes

Kids had some other ways to enjoy Rock Creek Park during its early history. For three decades beginning in 1904, Camp Goodwill gave low-income children and their mothers two-week outings scheduled throughout the summer — first at a site where the Rock Creek Golf Course is today and later at a tent city north of Fort DeRussy. Reflecting the shameful segregation of the times, Camp Goodwill was only open to white campers. African American children attended Camp Pleasant in Deanwood Heights.

All park areas today are closed to swimming and wading by both people and pets. But kids used to flock to Rock Creek's swimming holes until pollution concerns led to the posting of "No Bathing" signs in the 1920s and 30s. Popular swimming spots were found just north of Broad Branch, around the Joaquin Miller Cabin, near Kalmia Road and at "Big Rock" not far from Adams Mill. That last location was the favorite of *Evening Star* columnist John Clagett Proctor, who remembered:

> When Big Rock, in Rock Creek, was our bathing beach,
> And how we 'played hookey' its waters to reach.

An even older account dates way back to the 1850s, when a boy named Charles would go up the creek with his friends, "wading in it where we could not walk along the bank." As Charles recalled, they would "walk all over the Rock Creek country.... I became attached to almost every foot of it."

That boy grew up to become businessman Charles Glover, the prime mover behind the creation of Rock Creek Park in 1890.

As today's boys and girls wander through the same valley, where might a love of the Rock Creek wilderness take them?

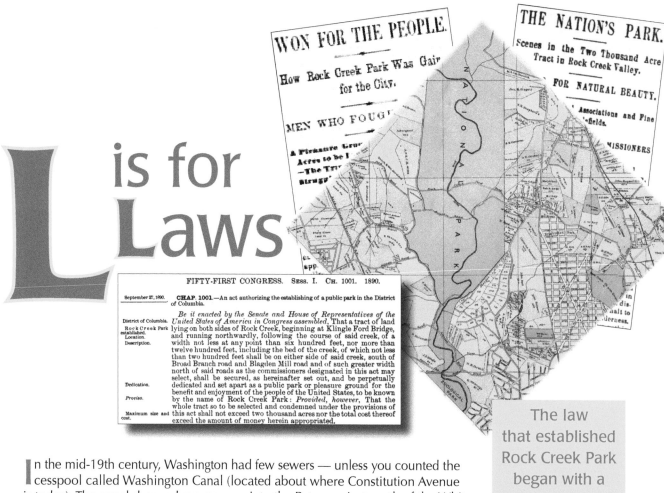

WON FOR THE PEOPLE.

How Rock Creek Park Was Gain
for the City.

MEN WHO FOUG

THE NATION'S PARK.

Scenes in the Two Thousand Acre
Tract in Rock Creek Valley.

FOR NATURAL BEAUTY.

Associations and Fine
fields.

MISSIONERS

FIFTY-FIRST CONGRESS. Sess. I. Ch. 1001. 1890.

September 27, 1890. **CHAP. 1001.**—An act authorizing the establishing of a public park in the District of Columbia.

Be it enacted by the Senate and House of Representatives of the United States of America in Congress assembled, That a tract of land lying on both sides of Rock Creek, beginning at Klingle Ford Bridge, and running northwardly, following the course of said creek, of a width not less at any point than six hundred feet, nor more than twelve hundred feet, including the bed of the creek, of which not less than two hundred feet shall be on either side of said creek, south of Broad Branch road and Blagden Mill road and of such greater width north of said roads as the commissioners designated in this act may select, shall be secured, as hereinafter set out, and be perpetually dedicated and set apart as a public park or pleasure ground for the benefit and enjoyment of the people of the United States, to be known by the name of Rock Creek Park: *Provided, however,* That the whole tract so to be selected and condemned under the provisions of this act shall not exceed two thousand acres nor the total cost thereof exceed the amount of money herein appropriated.

District of Columbia. Rock Creek Park established. Location. Description.

Dedication.

Proviso.

Maximum size and cost.

> The law
> that established
> Rock Creek Park
> began with a
> plan for a new
> White House.

In the mid-19th century, Washington had few sewers — unless you counted the cesspool called Washington Canal (located about where Constitution Avenue is today). The canal dumped raw sewage into the Potomac just south of the White House. The presidential mansion had other shortcomings. Not yet expanded with new wings, the modest building was a jumble of offices and living areas.

In 1866, the Senate ordered a study of possible new sites for an executive mansion to be surrounded by a buffer of parkland. When Major Nathaniel Michler of the US Army Corps of Engineers turned in his report the next year, his emphasis was on the green space, not the mansion.

Michler praised Rock Creek Valley as a "wild and romantic tract of country" worthy of a "national park." The Senate voted to acquire land for such a park. The House did not — and the moment passed.

The 1880s saw new interest in preserving the valley before developers could alter the natural landscape and possibly turn Rock Creek itself into something of a sewer. There was also a competing vision proposed in 1883 by Richard Hoxie, administrator of the city's sanitation system. While he too favored a large public park, he recommended as its centerpiece a lake four miles long that could satisfy DC's future water needs. Captain Hoxie proposed building a masonry dam above Georgetown to flood a large part of Rock Creek valley that he considered "nearly all of it worthless for any other purpose, being precipitous, rocky hillside."

Lobbying for Parkland

The city's business elite supported the preservation plan and rallied to find allies in Congress. Opponents resisted using taxpayer money for a park, especially after the federal government had to bail DC out of bankruptcy following Alexander Shepherd's aggressive spending on public improvements. Other detractors suggested that major park advocates — from Ohio Senator John Sherman to bankers Charles Glover and Brainard Warner — were only trying to get Uncle Sam to help increase the value of their own investments.

The Senate voted to establish the park in January 1890. Eying the upcoming 400th anniversary of Columbus' first voyage to America, the House added an amendment designating the preserve "Columbus Memorial Park"

— possibly attracting enough new votes to account for passage in April. A conference committee restored the name Rock Creek Park but retained a House provision requiring the District to pick up half the cost of purchasing land.

When President Benjamin Harrison signed the act into law September 27, 1890, only Yellowstone and Sequoia had been declared National Parks. Now Rock Creek joined them as "a public park or pleasure ground for the benefit and enjoyment of the people of the United States."

A Supreme Challenge

The legislation formed the new preserve mainly by condemning privately owned land. But it also mandated assessing owners of property adjoining the park for any resulting increase in value. Many of the same landowners who had lost part of their holdings to create the park (and had complained about inadequate compensation) found themselves with the prospect of higher assessments on their remaining property. They sued.

EXPLORING THE VALLEY.
The Rock Creek Park Commission on Its Travels.

THEY GO ON AN OBSERVATION TOUR ATTENDED BY A "STAR" REPORTER—INCIDENTS OF THE DAY—MEMBERS DELIGHTED WITH THE BEAUTY OF THE REGION.

The Rock Creek Park commission started out on a pilgrimage this morning to "view the landscape o'er," and if there was any of the landscape that was not included in the survey it will be hunted up some other day. Ten o'clock was the hour agreed upon for meeting, and Gen. Casey's house, 1419 K street, was the rendezvous. Two minutes before the appointed time Gen. H. V. Boynton and Mr. R. Ross Perry climbed the steps in front of 1419 and shook hands with Gen. Casey, who was on the lookout for his fellow-explorers. Five minutes later and two open carriages were driven to the sidewalk and there awaited

After the 1890 act was signed, the Rock Creek Commissioners made several expeditions to explore their new realm (left). They rode past the ruins of the Blagden Mill (above), which they later removed to make room for Beach Drive. The Supreme Court twice upheld the law—allowing the government to condemn and appraise private land (*Shoemaker v. US*, 1893) and assess adjoining property for increased value (*Wilson v. Lambert*, 1898, below).

It took the Supreme Court to decide in 1898 that such assessments were constitutional. But no extra taxes were ever paid. Although parkside property is highly valued today, the Rock Creek Commissioners determined that having a park next door had produced no appreciation in value.

More Laws Worth Celebrating

OCTOBER TERM, 1897.

WILSON v. LAMBERT.

APPEAL FROM THE COURT OF APPEALS OF THE DISTRICT OF COLUMBIA.

No. 164. Argued December 13, 14, 1897. — Decided January 3, 1898.

Opinion of the Court.

The sixth section of the act of September 27, 1890, c. 1001, 26 Stat. 492, authorizing the establishment of Rock Creek Park in the District of Columbia, does not violate the provisions of the Constitution of the United States, and is valid.

During the 40 years following the historic 1890 act, Congress passed several more laws with a significant impact on Rock Creek Park.

"An act to establish a National Park Service" was signed by President Woodrow Wilson in August 1916. However, Rock Creek Park did not come under its jurisdiction until a 1933 executive order from President Franklin Roosevelt.

A 1924 law created the National Capital Park Commission "to preserve the flow of water in Rock Creek, to prevent pollution of Rock Creek and the Potomac and Anacostia Rivers, to preserve forests and natural scenery in and about Washington, and to provide for the comprehensive ... development of the park, parkway, and playground system of the National Capital." The state of Maryland gave its own charter to the group in 1927 to acquire and administer parkland in Montgomery and Prince George's Counties — thereby establishing the Maryland-National Capital Park and Planning Commission.

Finally, the 1930 Capper-Cramton Act provided the basis for a huge expansion of protected land in the area, especially within the Rock Creek watershed. Michigan's Louis Cramton proposed generous federal grants and funding advances for the acquisition of parkland in DC and Maryland. The law led to the preservation of thousands of acres — including Rock Creek Regional Park in Maryland (under the MNCPPC) and such new parcels within Rock Creek Park as Potomac Palisades Parkway, the Fort Circle Parks and Melvin C. Hazen Park.

1890 law, 1890s Blagden Mill ruins: National Park Service; Real estate map, Fava Naeff & Co (1890): Library of Congress; *Won for the People* (10/4/1890), Exploring the Valley (10/18/1890): *Evening Star*; The Nation's Park (11/9/1890): *Pittsburg Dispatch*. *Wilson v. Lambert*: Davis, Putzel, Lind & Wagner, *Cases Adjudged in the Supreme Court*, vol. 168, Bank & Bros, 1898.

M is for Meridian Hill

With its expansive views overlooking downtown Washington and extending across the Potomac, Meridian Hill attracted ambitious plans over the years. It might have become the site of a new White House, the Vice President's home, the Lincoln Memorial, a Columbian Arch to rival the Arc de Triomphe, the Netherlands Carillon, the National Gallery of Art or the Naval Observatory.

Less than a mile from the natural wilderness of Rock Creek Valley, Rock Creek Park oversees a formal garden on Meridian Hill.

Remarkably, what did get built is as grand as any of the failed proposals — while still preserving the panorama. Meridian Hill Park was designed as a formal Italian Renaissance garden. Visitors wander along patterned walkways, descend dramatic stairways and duck into niches filled with benches and sculptures — as water splashes from fountains and tumbles downhill through 13 basins. People-watching is just as colorful, especially during the Sunday afternoon drum circles (left) held since the 1950s.

History on the Heights

Originally called Peter's Hill, the site was renamed Meridian Hill by Commodore David Porter after he purchased the property in 1816. The War of 1812 naval hero placed a stone marker on his land along a line directly north from the White House. President Thomas Jefferson had ordered the line drawn in 1804 to serve as the prime meridian of the District of Columbia or perhaps of the nation itself.

John Quincy Adams leased the estate after losing re-election in 1828. Leading up to the Civil War, the area was best known as a picnic spot. Meridian Hill housed military camps and army hospitals during the war. In 1867 the estate was among the first outside "Washington City" to be subdivided. African Americans who had found their way to the camps as free blacks and escaped slaves stayed on, purchasing land and building modest homes. The handsome Wayland Seminary at 15th and Euclid Streets educated black students, including Booker T. Washington.

Still, much of Meridian Hill remained forest and fields. Joaquin Miller, the colorful "Poet of the Sierras," lived in the neighborhood in a log cabin he constructed in 1883.

Becoming a High-Class Address

Former Senator John Henderson and his wife Mary Foote Henderson started buying land on Meridian Hill in 1888. They built for themselves a mansion of red sandstone known as Henderson Castle and erected elegant residential and embassy buildings nearby. Other developers followed suit, designing 15 Beaux Arts mansions for Meridian Hill by 1928.

Mrs. Henderson was a tireless promoter of many grand but unfulfilled proposals for the neighborhood. One plan that eventually did come to fruition — on land the couple sold to Congress in 1910 — was Meridian Hill Park.

Eventually took a long time. Only in 1936 could a *Washington Post* headline declare the park "Finally Completed after 26 Years of Hard Work, Petty Strife." The strife included a bitter congressional debate over whether James Buchanan deserved a monument, a proposal during World War I to sell the park or use it for war buildings and a constant struggle for appropriations.

A Park of Plenty

Washingtonians marveled at the result: a 12-acre garden fit for European royalty but open to all, featuring the nation's largest cascading fountain and the first use of concrete aggregate surfaces whose embedded pebbles created mosaic designs.

Statuary donated to beautify the park included the Buchanan statue, bequeathed by his niece and flanked by granite figures representing law and diplomacy; Joan of Arc, Washington's only equestrian statue of a woman, a gift from French women in New York to the women of America; a statue of Dante presented on the 600th anniversary of his death on behalf of Italian-Americans; "Serenity," sculpted from a white marble block in memory of a Navy officer; and a bronze armillary sphere 68 inches in diameter (now lost), bestowed to honor a local artist by her sister.

The open mall in the upper park was well-suited for concerts and gatherings. In the 1940s, the space hosted the Von Trapp Family, the Martha Graham Dancers and an annual program of chamber music. Plays were staged in a 917-seat theater over eight weeks in 1949 — in front of integrated audiences. The concert schedule ebbed during the 1950s and 60s, but included performances by the National Symphony and a 1968 gala that attracted up to 20,000 people.

Meridian Hill Park also became a place for activism, with some of the earliest rallies coming after the murder of Martin Luther King in 1968 and on the first anniversary of his assassination. Newspaper coverage of the 1969 rally recognized that the site was beginning to be called "Malcolm X Park," a name attributed to Angela Davis.

After crime and vandalism plagued the park during the 1970s and 80s, a group called Friends of Meridian Hill formed patrols, organized programs to attract visitors and helped the Park Service make improvements. The group was recognized at the White House in 1994, the same year Meridian Hill was designated a National Historic Landmark. Though it is not official, many use the double moniker, Meridian Hill/Malcolm X Park — recognizing both its grand history and its significance for the surrounding communities.

Today, with much of its infrastructure repaired and grace restored, Meridian Hill is once again a prime attraction and a neighborhood gem in the Rock Creek Park system.

The National Park Service website offers a cell phone audio tour with five stops in Meridian Hill Park (above). A bronze armillary sphere (left), designed to show the path of heavenly bodies, stood at the south end of the park until it was stolen during the 1970s.

The figure of Joan of Arc (below, and at #2 on the cell phone map) is a replica of a statue outside the Cathedral of Notre-Dame in Reims, France.

Cascade Fountain at Meridian Hill Park: Carol M. Highsmith Collection, Library of Congress; Cell phone map, Armillary sphere, Joan of Arc: National Park Service; Drum circle (David Swerdloff, 2015).

M also is for Mills

Over the course of 250 years, more than 20 mills relied on the water power of Rock Creek.

Rock Creek Valley was a high-tech corridor for 19th century Washington.

Using breakthroughs in automation, millwrights were able to tap the era's best energy source — the flow of water — to construct mills up and down Rock Creek. Mill owners further developed the region by building roads to connect their properties to area farms and to the few thoroughfares that led to the wharves of Georgetown and Washington city.

By mid-century, milling was the District's biggest industry. In addition to grist mills that made flour, other mills ground bone into fertilizer, carded wool, and turned out animal feed, paper, lumber or plaster.

Labor-saving Technology

Milling along Rock Creek had been a grueling business for more than a century, beginning in the late 1600s. Millers and their helpers hauled heavy sacks of wheat, corn and oats, manually sifted flour and packed it into bags and barrels. One of the earliest operations — White's Mill (later, Peters Mill) — took advantage of the strong rapids south of present-day Military Road. The creek also powered Lyons (or Federal) Mill on the opposite bank from Georgetown's Oak Hill Cemetery, Parrott's Mill a bit further south, Reed's and Deakins Mills by the mouth of Piney Branch, and the Patterson paper mill near P Street.

Then a Delaware visionary named Oliver Evans realized that gears, belts and pulleys could harness the movement of the mill's water wheel to do most of the back-breaking labor. Evans patented his methods and publicized them in a book printed in 1795, revolutionizing the industry.

Farmers who stepped into a mill built using Evans' system must have been dazzled by the constant motion, all happening automatically. Buckets arranged on conveyor belts lifted grain or flour from the basement to the attic, hoppers dropped precise amounts of grain onto millstones, mechanical rakes spread meal for drying, and rolling screens cleaned grain and sifted flour.

Many of the Rock Creek mills provided custom milling for neighboring farmers, who paid with a portion of their grain. The alternative, grinding flour for export, put mill owners in competition with large operations established along the Potomac River and the Chesapeake and Ohio Canal, where barges could be used to transport grain and flour.

Lyons Mill (top, in 1908) was constructed above Georgetown around 1780 and remained in operation for 95 years. Blagden's Mill, shown in ruins in the 1890s, was built using innovative designs (example at left) published in 1795 by Oliver Evans, who automated much of the labor of milling.

For Some, a Profit Stream

No less a luminary than John Quincy Adams discovered that Rock Creek did not always provide a good flow of cash. One year before becoming President, he purchased the Columbian Mill on land that is now part of the National Zoo — but in the end pronounced it "a losing concern." The name Columbian was inherited from an earlier mill built on the site before 1800 in what was then the newly established District of Columbia.

Argyle Mill and Peirce Mill had greater commercial success — and the same man is credited with building both of these neighboring mills. As millwright Isaac Peirce began acquiring property in Rock Creek Valley, he purchased Deakins Mill in 1794, which he replaced by building the state-of-the-art Peirce Mill in the 1820s. Because of a legal dispute over ownership of the Argyle estate just up the creek, Peirce was unable to purchase that property. But it's likely he was hired to construct Argyle Mill on the parcel sometime before 1800 — allowing him to try out the new technology before erecting his own mill.

Argyle Mill became known as Blagden's Mill after Thomas Blagden bought the estate in 1853. By 1860 his mill was turning out 4,200 barrels of flour per year. Meanwhile, over at Peirce Mill, as many as 12 wagonloads of wheat would arrive each day for grinding. To provide access to their businesses, the Peirce family laid out Peirce Mill Road and Joshua Peirce's (Klingle) Road in 1831, followed by Broad Branch Road in 1839. Blagden's Mill (originally Argyle Mill) Road was built privately in 1847.

Rock Creek also boasted at least 10 more mills upstream in Maryland with such familiar names as Jones Mill, Plyer's Mill, Veirs Mill and Muncaster Mill (which, in 1925, was the creek's last commercial mill).

Mills End

By the late 19th century, newer technology was making the mills obsolete, including the use of metal rollers instead of millstones, rail transportation and steam power. As government became Washington's primary industry, grain production declined. Some of the mills were done in by the very creek that made them possible. The Johnstown Flood of 1889 devastated Blagden's Mill, whose ruins were removed during the construction of Beach Drive, and also washed away the remains of Adams Mill, which had closed in 1867.

Peirce Mill survived the flood and continued to make flour until the main shaft broke in 1897. Symbolically, its final millers — brothers Charles and Alciblades White — were descendants of the man who built White's Mill in the early days of Rock Creek milling.

Peirce Mill was restored in the 1930s and continued operating until 1958 to demonstrate a piece of local history — and provide flour to government cafeterias during World War II. Another renovation kept the millwheel turning from 1970 to 1993. After the latest reconstruction, undertaken by the Friends of Peirce Mill, the mill resumed grinding grain in 2011 — allowing today's Washingtonians to experience one of the technological marvels of the 19th century.

Peirce Mill (right) has been restored to operation three times during Rock Creek Park history. In 1937, after the first renovation, the mill began selling flour and cornmeal to government cafeterias and the public. Raymond Watt (above, filling bags of freshly ground grain) was miller from 1940 to 1966. Sales resumed in the 1970s after the second restoration—though they are forbidden today due to sanitary concerns.

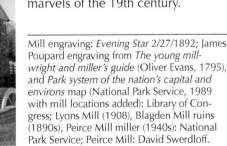

Mill engraving: *Evening Star* 2/27/1892; James Poupard engraving from *The young millwright and miller's guide* (Oliver Evans, 1795), and *Park system of the nation's capital and environs* map (National Park Service, 1989 with mill locations added): Library of Congress; Lyons Mill (1908), Blagden Mill ruins (1890s), Peirce Mill miller (1940s): National Park Service; Peirce Mill: David Swerdloff.

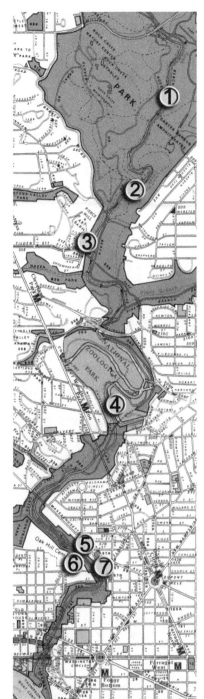

The location of major mills along Rock Creek, including some sites that housed additional mills producing paper, plaster, fertilizer, wool or lumber:

1- White's (later, Peters), 1759 or so to early 1800s;
2- Argyle (called Blagden after 1853), late 1790s to 1889;
3- Reed's (1747) and Deakins (1790) replaced in 1820s by Peirce;
4- Columbian (called Adams after 1825), pre-1790 to 1818 (burned down) then 1818 to 1867;
5- Lyons (or Federal), 1780 to 1875;
6- Parrott's (carded and spun wool in early 1800s);
7- Patterson (later Columbia Paper Mill of Rock Creek), 1800 to after 1868.

N

Drains To Rock Creek

is for Neighbor

O ne yard at a time, Washington area residents are protecting the environment of Rock Creek Park.

They act because — even with the best stewardship of the National Park Service — only efforts across the entire region can keep the Park from being beset by invasive plants, poisons and sediment in its streams, periodic flooding and a loss of wildlife.

Garden Responsibly

Roughly 300 of the 700 plant species within Rock Creek Park are non-native invasives. As these intruders grow out of control, they crowd out native plants — often without providing food for creatures and birds. The problem is so great that eradication projects are focused in just two areas: the mature tree canopy and habitats with the highest biodiversity. Even these efforts are undermined when people possibly miles away use non-native species in their landscaping. The invasives keep showing up in the park — spread by air, water, wild animals, birds, the dumping of yard waste and hitchhiking on the clothing, shoes and pets of park visitors.

Good neighbors are removing invasive vines, grasses, shrubs and trees from their yards and planting native species that are just as attractive and more sustainable. Some people are going further by combining native plantings into a backyard wildlife habitat that offers food, water and shelter to a variety of animals, native and migrating birds, pollinators and other beneficial insects, and even helpful bacteria and fungi. Adding trees to the overall canopy also helps moderate the climate for the entire region.

Anyone in the 77 square miles of the Rock Creek watershed can be a good neighbor to the Park.

Use This, Not That

Naturalists can recommend specific native vegetation to take the place of invasives — as they remind us how harmful popular alien species can be.

For example, the European import called lesser celandine (fig buttercup) has beautiful yellow blooms. Yet the plant is among the first to emerge in forested floodplains, creating an impenetrable carpet (left, below) that can nearly erase from the calendar the arrival of native wildflowers in the spring. Instead, try planting spotted geranium (left, above), wild ginger or foam flower.

Use native honeysuckles and not the exotic varieties whose fruit does not support migrating birds — or plant spicebush, arrow wood or swamp rose. Destroy the English ivy and porcelainberry vines that can become so weighty they often uproot trees — and bring in Virginia creeper, creeping phlox or lady fern.

Environmentalists also have a special disdain for Tree of Heaven, the species celebrated in the novel, *A Tree Grows in Brooklyn* (and one we might more easily resist if we called it by its alternate name, stinking sumac). True to the book, the tree grows tenaciously. But it also produces chemicals that kill nearby vegetation and prevent new growth. Preferred substitutes include native sumacs, oaks, box elder and black walnut.

A Department of Agriculture landscape architect demonstrates a rain barrel outside USDA headquarters in 2012.

Calming the Storm

Neighbors can't stop the rain — but they can keep some of it from running off their roofs, driveways and lawns into storm drains. Whatever flows from our yards joins with water coming off streets and buildings to sweep trash, sediment and toxic chemicals all the way to Rock Creek. Fast-flowing water also erodes the banks of the creek and its tributaries.

To stem this flood, residents are installing rain barrels, cisterns and dry wells. They are creating rain gardens, installing green roofs and replacing impermeable pavement. Their communities are posting reminders on storm drains that anything dumped there ends up in Rock Creek.

You Are Not Alone

You can find help reshaping your own environment to protect the overall ecology of Rock Creek Park.

Under an initiative by Rock Creek Conservancy called *Rock Creek Park In Your Backyard*, experts will visit your yard and prepare a site report. Together you can set goals aimed at removing invasives, planting native species, creating a rich wildlife habitat and reducing stormwater runoff. Hitting different benchmarks will result in Silver, Gold or Platinum Status for each yard — along with an attractive yard sign and other perks.

Volunteers prepare a place for one of 35 trees donated by Casey Trees in 2010 as part of an annual planting partnership with DC's Crestwood neighborhood adjoining Rock Creek Park.

Programs like RiverSmart Homes in the District and Rain-Scapes Rewards in Montgomery County can prescribe ways to keep rainwater from flowing from your yard into storm drains, and they'll help install and pay for the improve-ments. Casey Trees will rebate part of the cost of new trees and assist in choosing the right tree in the right spot. The group also offers communities the chance to organize as a neighborhood for free tree plantings. Maryland's WildAcres program has several fact sheets on landscaping that attracts wildlife. And one recommended site that matches your yard to local plant species is nativeplantcenter.net.

Using these resources, area residents can each do a little bit toward making a big difference. The wild ribbon of green we call Rock Creek Park cannot thrive without the vigilance of its neighbors.

Storm drain mural, 2014: Rock Creek Conservancy; Spotted geranium (Jennifer Anderson): USDA Natural Resources Conservation Service PLANTS database; *Invasive Lesser Celandine* (Sam Sheline, 2014) courtesy of NatureServe and Rain barrel (Bob Nichols, 2012)/USDA, both via flickr.com under Creative Commons 2.0 license and cropped; Tree planting: Crestwood Citizens Assn.

O is for Olmsted

Many of Washington's natural wonders — including its largest park — owe much of their appearance and existence to the work of two men named Frederick Law Olmsted.

The senior Olmsted practically invented the field of American landscape architecture beginning with his plan for New York's Central Park in the 1850s. He championed the idea of the public park as a common green space accessible to all. In an urbanizing America, parkland was to serve both the body and the spirit. In design, all parts of the landscape were to be in harmony, with no detail standing out.

The junior Olmsted followed in his father's footsteps and philosophy. Along the way, he created the first comprehensive plan for Rock Creek Park some 28 years after it was established.

> The first family of American landscape architecture shaped the design of Rock Creek Park.

Mr. Olmsted Comes to Washington

In DC, the elder Frederick Law Olmsted is most celebrated for designing the Capitol grounds between 1874 and 1892. He also supported plans to create Rock Creek Park, warning in 1886 that "the charmingly wooded glen of Rock Creek" was "in private hands, subject any day to be laid waste." He turned his attention to one slice of the valley in 1890. Working in partnership with his adopted son (and nephew) John Charles Olmsted, he designed the National Zoological Park, whose main thoroughfare is named Olmsted Walk in their honor.

As failing health forced Olmsted to retire in 1895, he brought into the firm his 25-year-old son, Frederick Law Olmsted Jr. The young man, known familiarly as "Rick," quickly proved himself. In 1898 the company was renamed Olmsted Brothers, with Rick and John Charles as partners.

The McMillan Report

Olmsted Jr. became a leading advocate for one of his father's causes: to re-establish and extend L'Enfant's plan for the nation's capital. He took what would have been his father's place on a Senate panel known as the McMillan Commission. Their 1902 report set out to restore the Mall, which had become cluttered with a market, a railway station and a series of Victorian parks. But Olmsted also encouraged the commission to endorse the acquisition of land for new public parks and scenic drives throughout the city — including the preservation of the entire Rock Creek valley.

Olmsted remained a steward of the commission's recommendations, first as part of an unpaid but influential group of consultants and then as a charter member of two federal oversight boards, the Commission of Fine Arts and the National Capital Park and Planning Commission. His battles at the CFA, especially to resist relocating the Botanic Garden in Rock Creek Park, convinced Olmsted that the park needed a far-reaching plan — and that Olmsted Brothers should prepare it.

The result was a 1918 report whose guiding principle mandated that the "interesting, varied, natural scenery must be saved intact insofar as possible," though it could be "restored or perfected by intelligent, appreciative landscape development."

Another fundamental consideration was access to and through the park. Yet all roads and paths — as well as bridges, benches and other structures — "should fit into the landscape as harmonious and subordinate parts of the scenery."

The Olmsted Brothers' 1918 report praised the park's valley scenes for "ever stimulating the desire to explore beyond the next turn."

One Park, Six Settings

The 1918 report divided Rock Creek Park into six types of naturalistic landscapes that remain familiar today (see map below). The area along the banks of Rock Creek and its tributaries was described as "topographically and psychologically the backbone … of the Park." This "Valley Section" was to be preserved in its natural state, with the addition of little more than a few picnic spots.

The hills and plateaus west of Rock Creek and south of Military Road were termed Woodland for Intensive Use. The report recommended the installation of hiking paths, a roadway along the ridgeline and numerous picnic groves. In contrast, much of the forest north of Military Road was designated "Wilder Woodland" and was to be "preserved to the highest degree."

Old farm fields north of Military Road made up the "Open Hillside Section." Its grassy slopes were to be maintained and adorned with occasional shade trees and overlooks to create "a sense of freedom, breadth, and outlook found nowhere else in the Park."

At the northern tip, the "Meadow Park" — a section of flat meadow surrounded by forest — was to be preserved as another unique landscape.

Finally, the report recognized the area along 16th Street and Colorado Avenue as being "separated topographically from the rest of the Park." Instead of being kept wild, this "Plateau Recreation Ground" was to be adapted for recreational activities from sports to band concerts. At the time, the plateau was already the site of playing fields, tennis courts and horse shows.

Following his work on the Rock Creek report, Rick Olmsted continued to influence the design of Washington landmarks from the White House grounds and the Jefferson Memorial to Theodore Roosevelt Island and the gardens of the National Cathedral. When he died in 1957, landscape architects with the name Frederick Law Olmsted had been working for a full 100 years to bring parkland to the people.

Today we see the Olmsteds' legacy in the varied landscapes of Rock Creek Park, in the green vistas that soothe our spirits and in the roads and paths that provide such easy access into nature.

This enhanced version of a map in the 1918 report locates six different landscapes within the park. The report also recommended the construction of two high-level "viaduct crossings" (shown in silver) to prevent "the intrusion into the very heart of the Park of the noise and tangle of heavy trucks and electric [street]cars."

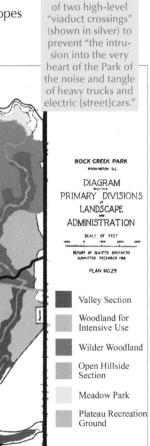

ROCK CREEK PARK
WASHINGTON D.C.

DIAGRAM
PRIMARY DIVISIONS
of
LANDSCAPE
and
ADMINISTRATION

SCALE OF FEET

REPORT OF OLMSTED BROTHERS
SUBMITTED DECEMBER 1918

PLAN NO.29

■ Valley Section

Woodland for Intensive Use

Wilder Woodland

Open Hillside Section

Meadow Park

Plateau Recreation Ground

Frederick Law Olmsted by John Singer Sargent (1895): Wikimedia Commons; Frederick Law Olmsted Jr.: National Park Service; Beach Drive photo: David Swerdloff; Rock Creek photo: Lorraine Swerdloff; Map: Rock Creek Park Report (Olmsted Brothers, 1918): NPS (with added color and legend).

P is for Peirce

This painting from the early 1830s captures Peirce Mill and Peirce's Mill Road shortly after both were constructed. In the foreground a horse rider uses a ford to cross Rock Creek.

Quarrying stone. Building mills that ground wheat and corn for area farmers. Growing grain, hay, potatoes and peas. Planting and harvesting orchards of fruit trees. Raising pigs, sheep and dairy cows. Making brandy. Felling trees for lumber. Marketing plants of all kinds. These are some of the commercial activities the Peirce family pursued on their property on the banks of Rock Creek.

The story involves three families who left Quaker settlements in Pennsylvania. Skilled millwright Isaac Peirce arrived in the mid-1780s. He worked with his wife's brothers, Amos and Abner Cloud, as the families purchased land in Maryland and Virginia. Another family, the Shoemakers, began moving to Washington in 1800.

The history of the Peirce family reveals Rock Creek Valley as a place of commerce during the 19th century.

The Peirce Plantation

Isaac Peirce amassed property along Rock Creek, starting with the purchase in 1794 of 160 acres that included a house, barn, mill, slave quarters and hundreds of fruit trees. Small boats would carry plaster up the creek to be ground at his mill. Isaac added a saw mill around 1800. Using stone quarried along Broad or Piney Branch, he then constructed a spring house, carriage house, distillery and — by 1829 — a new mill based on recent revolutionary designs.

Map showing part of the Peirce family properties along Rock Creek in the late 1850s. On the left, Peirce Mill and some of the fields and orchards overseen by Pierce Shoemaker. On the right, Joshua Peirce's Linnaean Hill estate with its winding paths designed to show off the landscaping plants he cultivated and sold.

Historians believe Isaac had earlier built the nearly identical Argyle mill just up the creek on land he was unable to secure for himself. Beginning in 1853, when the Blagdens purchased that mill and an adjoining 300-acre estate, their farming and milling business was second in the valley only to the Peirces'. Meanwhile, Abner Cloud and Jonathan Shoemaker also owned mills, one near present-day Fletcher's Boathouse, the other downstream from the Peirce farmstead. Neither was profitable. However, Jonathan's nephew David did succeed in marrying Isaac Peirce's daughter Abigail in 1815.

As Isaac Peirce became one of Washington's primary landowners, he began leasing out Peirce Mill to concentrate on the family's other economic pursuits: real estate, farming, raising animals and making cider and brandy. Upon his death, the mill and most of his property went to elder son Abner, who himself died ten years later. Running the family business fell to David and Abigail's son, Pierce Shoemaker. The mill remained a money-maker. But, like his father-in-law, Shoemaker sought a bigger return from other pursuits, increasing the amount of cultivated land by 50 percent to 120 acres, expanding the timber business to supply a growing city and dealing in real estate.

Isaac Peirce's younger son, Joshua, had taken an interest in his father's orchards. In 1823, Isaac gave Joshua 82 acres, which he renamed Linnaean Hill — after Carl Linnaeus, who invented the system of classifying living things by genus and species. Joshua then went into the nursery business, publishing catalogs of trees, plants and flowers and marketing over a number of states. He helped introduce Americans to exotic imports, especially camellias. He created a landscaped "pleasure garden" to lure customers to his business in what was still fairly remote countryside — but also opened a city branch off 14th Street. And he constructed a hilltop mansion made of that same Rock Creek stone.

Despite their Quaker roots, the families relied on slave labor for some five decades. Slaves owned by the Peirces and Shoemakers worked as house servants, farm laborers, coachmen and salesmen. One of them, William H. Becket, was foreman of Joshua Peirce's nursery business.

When emancipation was declared in DC in 1862, Pierce Shoemaker applied for compensation for 20 slaves. Joshua Peirce's petition listed 11, include Becket. After the Civil War, Joshua brought Becket back as an employee, and the former slave was at his side when he died in 1869. Even without slave labor, the Peirces and Shoemakers continued to prosper, and Pierce Shoemaker built a handsome home called Cloverdale up the hill from the old family cottage.

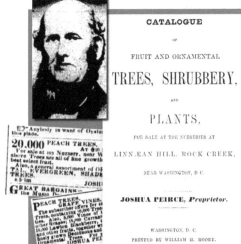

Joshua Peirce (above) marketed his nursery business with catalogs and ads for "20,000 Peach Trees." The Peirce family controlled many hundreds of acres in Rock Creek Valley and beyond. In the 1870 Census (below), the listing for "farmer" Pierce Shoemaker showed real estate worth $112,535 and more than $7,200 in personal property.

3	4	5	6	7	8	9
Shoemaker Pierce	56	M	W	Farmer	112535	7265
" Lewis P.	14	M	W			
" Caroline M.	13	F	W			
" Francis T.	10	M	W			

Business Grinds to a Halt

Shoemaker's nephew, Joshua Peirce Klingle, inherited Linnaean Hill — which explains why the home Joshua Peirce constructed came to be known as Klingle Mansion. More interested in real estate and politics, Klingle closed down the nursery business. By the 1880s, commerce was also winding down on the Peirce plantation. Milling had become unprofitable, as the number of farms plummeted and newer methods produced flour more cheaply. Peirce Mill became more famous as a picnic destination.

Even before the main shaft at Peirce Mill broke in 1897, the mill had become a picturesque destination for country outings. These visitors (c. 1920) may have gone to the teahouse that operated in the building from 1905 to 1933.

The decline of commerce helped turn attention to the Peirce land as a recreation destination and eventually to the establishment of Rock Creek Park. Pierce Shoemaker's son, Louis, did lead an energetic resistance when the park law was signed in 1890 — challenging the right of the government to take his land and the amount of money received in return. But, after losing these battles, he became a supporter of preservation within the park and a civic leader in the Brightwood neighborhood.

Many of the Peirce family buildings remain today: Peirce Mill, Klingle Mansion, Cloverdale, the spring house, the carriage house and the distillery (now part of a private home). The newly restored mill resumed grinding grain in 2011 — and offers a regular schedule of milling demonstrations. Friends of Peirce Mill and Casey Trees (two non-profit groups that support the National Park Service) have planted a small orchard as a reminder of the brisk economic activity beyond milling that took place along Rock Creek during the 1800s and further added to the authenticity of Peirce Mill.

Peirce Mill painting (artist unknown) and Joshua Peirce photo: National Park Service; *Topographical Map of the District of Columbia Surveyed in the Years 1856-59 by A. Boschke* (McClelland Blanchard & Mohun, DC, 1861): Library of Congress; 1857 Catalog and Peirce Mill photo (1918-1920): LOC; 1870 Census: ancestry.com; Nursery ads: *Evening Star* 11/7/1857, 3/17/1862.

Q is for Quotations

As one of Washington's most cherished spaces, Rock Creek has frequently attracted presidential attention. Woodrow Wilson wrote, "That park is the most beautiful thing in the United States." Theodore Roosevelt recalled that "each Sunday afternoon the whole family spent in Rock Creek Park, which was then very real country indeed." John Quincy Adams sought relaxation from his official duties in "this romantic glen, listening to the singing of a thousand birds."

Rock Creek Park has inspired natives and newcomers, poets and politicians to praise its scenery as "wild and rugged" and "blushing with beauty."

On the other hand, the creek has also been called "foul-smelling [and] mud-laden." And, when the Washington, DC-based Blackbyrds put a song called "Rock Creek Park" on the charts in 1976 (peaking at #37 R&B), they disregarded the ubiquitous "Closed at Dusk" signs to praise "doing it in the park, doing it after dark, oh yeah, Rock Creek Park."

Here are some notable quotations about our urban oasis:

"To Rock Creek there is nothing comparable in any capital city in Europe. What city in the world is there where a man ... can within ... a quarter of an hour on his own feet get into a beautiful rocky glen, such as you would find in the woods of Maine or Scotland ... with a broad stream foaming over its stony bed and wild, leafy woods looking down on each side?

British Ambassador to the United States, Lord James Bryce, 1913

"This wild and romantic tract of country ... with its charming drives and walks, its hills and dales, its pleasant valleys and deep ravines, its primeval forests and cultivated fields, its running waters, its rocks clothed with rich fern and mosses, its repose and tranquility, its light and shade, its ever-varying shrubbery, its beautiful and extensive views ... there you can find nature diversified in almost every hue and form.

Major Nathaniel Michler, early advocate for Rock Creek Park, in a letter to Missouri Senator B. Gratz Brown, 1867

"It has running water; it has rugged hills; it has picturesque scenery; it has abundance of varied forest timber; it has a native undergrowth blushing with beauty; it has the tangled vine and the clustering wildflower, and the quiet mosses gray with age, and indeed a thousand imprints of native adornment that no hand of art could ever equal in its most imitative mood.

Senator Brown, Chairman of the Public Buildings and Grounds Committee, 1867

No matter how perfect the scenery of the Park may be or may become, no matter how high its potential value, that value remains potential except insofar as it is enjoyed by large and ever larger numbers of people, poor and rich alike.

Olmsted Brothers, 1918

Rock Creek has an abundance of all the elements that make up not only pleasing but wild and rugged scenery. There is perhaps, not another city in the Union that has on its very threshold so much natural beauty and grandeur, such as men seek for in remote forests and mountains.

American naturalist John Burroughs, 1868

A wonder of the simple time of old
When machines were of the rarest mark.
So we of these enlightened times
See once again as our forefathers saw
And hear old Pierce's mill at work again ...

*Interior Department employee
Walter Hough, 1935*

It is hard to believe that the foul-smelling, mud-laden, debris-choked watercourse which winds its sickly way from Montgomery County, Maryland through the nation's capital can be the same stream which Major Michler described ... some 90 years ago."

Bernard Frank, US Forest Service, 1954

Rock Creek, like the city of Washington, belongs to all the people of America. We must ask ourselves how can we expect to clean up any river in the nation, if we cannot clean up Rock Creek Park?

US Interior Secretary Stewart Udall, 1967

Oak, tulip poplar, beech & laurel
holly, dogwood on the hills,
sycamore, red maple, wet,
tolerant, all along the floodplain
through steep ravines, gentle
sloping hills, grassy meadows
and the stretch of rapids
south of Military Road,
the Secession War captured in
 a street sign
now as frenzied commuter route
where 20,000 years ago
nomads sharpened fluted points
for caribou, elk, moose,
black bear, mastodon & mammoth

*Poet and English professor Joshua
Weiner, from "Rock Creek (II)"
(The Figure of a Man Being Swallowed
by a Fish, University of Chicago
Press, 2013), used with permission
of the author*

Whoever heard of the falls of Rock creek? At the distance of about four miles from the city and within the limits of the District lie these beautiful, wild and romantic falls, unknown and unfrequented in a deep glen, surrounded by lofty hills on either side.... Here, Nature as though expressly for the accommodation of picnic parties, has constructed tables from her everlasting rocks and surrounded them with ottomans that would well adorn the portico or even the parlor of a prince.

*Joshua Peirce, owner of
"Linnaean Hill," 1835*

Palm Warbler migrating through
Rock Creek Park and strollers in snow:
Matthew Sileo/MatthewSileoPhotog-
raphy.com; other Rock Creek scenes:
David and Lorraine Swerdloff.

WARNING!
Sewage
Avoid contact with river after rain.

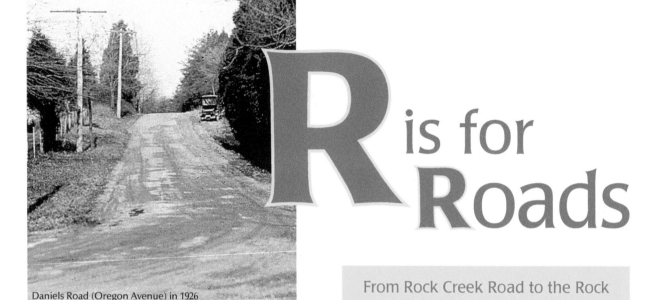

R is for Roads

Daniels Road (Oregon Avenue) in 1926

From Rock Creek Road to the Rock Creek and Potomac Parkway, traffic has traveled on roads to Rock Creek Valley over parts of four centuries.

Much of what we now call Washington was given the name Rock Creek Hundred back in 1715. The name of the creek was then applied to a parish and a church — and eventually to a road that led to the church and continued to the upper Rock Creek Valley. This first route north into the wilderness endures on modern maps as Columbia Road, Rock Creek Church Road and Blair Road — and St. Paul's Rock Creek Church still stands on land donated in 1719.

Another early road proceeded west from the church to cross Rock Creek at the shallowest point in the upper valley. Few remnants remain of Milkhouse Ford Road — mainly the park trail west from the ford and three city blocks called Rock Creek Ford Road.

PINEY BRANCH BRIDGE

Road System of the 19th Century

The mid-1800s saw the first road out of the city to pass through what would become Rock Creek Park: a narrow and hilly country way called Piney Branch Road (or, sometimes, 14th Street Road). The route descended to Piney Branch creek from Mount Pleasant. Then — before climbing steeply through the present-day Crestwood neighborhood — it crossed the stream over a rickety bridge (left) just west of where the 16th Street "Tiger" Bridge finally succeeded in spanning Piney Branch Valley in the early 20th century. Piney Branch Road was an alternative to 7th Street Road (today's Georgia Avenue, which earlier had been a turnpike and a "plank road" lined with hemlock boards).

Other roads built before the Civil War served the valley's mills and farms: Peirce's Mill Road (1831), Klingle Ford Road (1831) and Linnean Hill Road were laid out privately to provide access to Peirce family holdings — and have been largely replaced by Tilden Street, Klingle Road and Park Road. Adams Mill Road and Blagden's Mill Road (1847) served mills down and upstream. Broad Branch Road (1839) followed a Rock Creek tributary and, like Peirce's Mill Road, led to the road to Frederick (now Wisconsin Avenue).

Other roads built before Rock Creek Park was founded bore the names of property owners Swart, Daniels and Moreland (now 27th Street, Oregon and Utah Avenues respectively). By 1864, the old roads were brought into the DC system and Military Road was constructed to connect the forts defending the capital.

New Park, New Roads

The 1890 law establishing Rock Creek Park instructed the Army Corps of Engineers to "lay out and prepare roadways." From 1897 to 1900 the Corps' Capt. Lansing Beach built the road that would be named in his honor: Beach Drive. With Congress slow to approve appropriations, Beach began by using prison labor and letting park tenants provide work in place of rent.

By the end of the 1920s, the park's transportation system had expanded to include roads named after other Army engineers (Bingham, Grant, Morrow, Sherrill) and park leaders (Ross, Joyce). Wise Road took its name from a nearby dairy farm. Glover Road honors Charles Glover, the businessman who led the push to create the park.

Piney Branch Parkway was authorized in 1907, but not built until the mid-1930s when funding and workers became available through the New Deal. The road was intended to honor another Corps engineer, but the name Biddle Parkway never caught on.

A slow trickle of appropriations also delayed construction of the Rock Creek and Potomac Parkway. Approved in 1913, it wasn't completed until 1936. By that time, the route designed to bring people into parkland was viewed more as a commuter highway to bring workers into the city. The parkway became one-way during rush hours in 1937.

Expressway To Controversy

Some officials proposed extending the parkway up Rock Creek as an expressway. Heated debate delayed construction of a tunnel leading north from the parkway that would circumvent two fords near the zoo. Though no superhighway was ever approved, the tunnel didn't open until 1966 (dedication ceremony, left).

The issues raised presaged continuing controversies over the roads of Rock Creek Park. What is the proper balance between the needs of drivers and the protection of the park's environment and peaceful setting — also taking into account appeals for better bicycle access? Olmsted Brothers anticipated the dilemma in the 1918 plan for Rock Creek Park, saying it "must be opened up to the driving, riding, and walking public; but the roads … must be … so built that the essential qualities of the Park are impaired in the least possible degree."

Daniels Road, tunnel dedication photos: National Park Service; Map adapted from District of Columbia topographic map, US Coast & Geodetic Survey 1892-94 (engraved by Evans & Bartle, DC): Library of Congress; Bridge engraving: *Evening Star*, 9/5/1891.

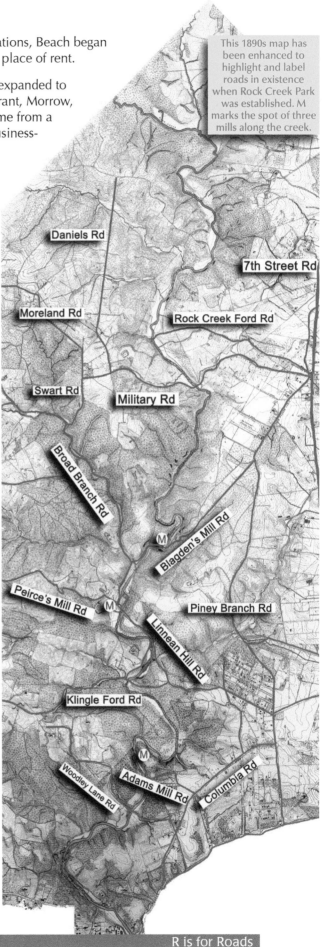

This 1890s map has been enhanced to highlight and label roads in existence when Rock Creek Park was established. M marks the spot of three mills along the creek.

Daniels Rd

7th Street Rd

Moreland Rd

Rock Creek Ford Rd

Swart Rd

Military Rd

Broad Branch Rd

M

Blagden's Mill Rd

Peirce's Mill Rd

M

Piney Branch Rd

Linnean Hill Rd

Klingle Ford Rd

M

Woodley Lane Rd

Adams Mill Rd

Columbia Rd

S is for Sports

Throughout the year, sports enthusiasts enjoy the courts, courses, fields and trails of Rock Creek Park.

The athletes of Rock Creek Park have ranged from hikers and rollerbladers to world champions in tennis, golf and bicycle racing. Summertime visitors rent watercraft at the mouth of the creek at Thompson Boat Center. Winter storms attract cross-country skiers, who may be cheered to know the park holds the DC record for deepest snowfall (33 inches in 1922). Once or twice a year, the creek may flow high enough to allow brave kayakers to venture out.

From the beginning, the park's wild environment provided the perfect setting for hiking, horseback riding and — until the streams became too polluted and fishing was prohibited north of Porter Street — swimming and angling. Ice skaters used to gather after a hard freeze at a shallow section of the creek near the National Zoo. Formal hiking and bridle paths were added in the early 20th century. Equestrians took advantage of the Equitation Field beginning in the 1930s and a modern horse center starting in 1972.

Foot and Pedal Power

Today, typical half-day loop hikes from the Nature Center take you past the creek's wildest whitewater, historic bridges and fords, Civil War defenses and even a stack of cement pieces once part of the US Capitol. Or make your own way along any of the blazed trails, including the Valley Trail that stretches from the Jusserand Memorial near Park Road north to the marshland by Boundary Bridge at the DC/Maryland line. Even a brief ramble along a park trail will help you connect with nature in the middle of the city.

Bicycle riders pedaled the scenic country roads in and around Rock Creek Valley before the park was established. The first paved bike paths didn't appear until the 1960s, when the National Park Service also began testing the idea of closing parts of Beach Drive to motor traffic. A Sunday auto-ban became permanent in 1972, with Saturdays and holidays added in 1981. Nearly the entire park was shut down in June 1978 for America's first international bicycle event in 66 years — the Junior World Cycling Championships.

The park's bicycle routes connect with the Capital Crescent Trail (paved) and Georgetown Branch Trail (crushed gravel) to create a 21-mile circuit through scenic and historic landscapes (along with a few coffeeshops). Capital Bikeshare also makes bicycles available at several locations near the park.

Playing on the Plateau

The park became the home of organized sports after the Brightwood Reservoir opened near 16th Street and Colorado Avenue in 1900. When park authorities (under pressure from Congress) allowed the DC Water Department to use the parcel, they were

Gael Monfils of France competes in the finals of the 2011 pro tournament at the Fitzgerald Tennis Stadium.

Runners pick up the pace along Rock Creek Parkway in the 2005 Marine Corps Marathon (above). Three golfers in 1924 take on what was then a nine-hole course (below).

agreeing for the first time not to preserve a section of the park in its natural state. The decision was made easier because the reservoir was located on an isolated plateau just 300 yards south of a working racetrack. Horse races continued at the track until 1909 — and the venue also hosted occasional baseball games, bicycle competitions and Washington's first automobile races.

Once the precedent was set to allow the reservoir, it seemed natural to use the rest of the plateau for recreation. A nine-hole golf course was laid out in 1907, though never completed. Playing fields and tennis courts were built in 1916. More space became available after the reservoir was bulldozed in 1937. Today the fields at 16th and Kennedy Streets can be reserved through DC's Department of Parks and Recreation for use by soccer, football, baseball, field hockey and other sports teams.

Courts on the plateau began hosting pro tennis tournaments in 1969. The William H. G. Fitzgerald Tennis Stadium opened in 1987 (to the delight of Andre Agassi, who won the singles title five times). Women's play was added to the tournament in 2012. The annual event supports the Washington Tennis and Education Foundation's programs to help the lives of under-served DC youngsters.

Putters and Paddlers

The park finally did get its public golf course in the 1920s — over the protests of former President Woodrow Wilson, who called plans for a course "an unforgivable piece of vandalism." The links were forced to shrink by about 25 percent during the 1950s due to the construction of Joyce Road and the addition of new lanes to Military Road. Other recreation facilities built along Rock Creek include the Thompson Boat Center (1960) — home base for rowing clubs and crews from area high schools and universities — and the Park Road tennis courts (1926).

On a typical weekend, you can now find people pursuing all of their favorite sports. Hikers and horse riders follow wooded trails. Bicyclists wheel along paved paths. Golf and tennis enthusiasts aim for their personal best. Teams compete on playing fields. Frisbees fly at picnic areas. And the section of Beach Drive closed to traffic attracts a colorful congregation of visitors, both on foot and using non-motorized contraptions that range from in-line skates and recumbent bikes to tricycles for kids and wheeled carriers for dogs. Rock Creek Park can give anybody a sporting chance.

T is for Trees

When Rock Creek Park was established in 1890, urban parks and national parks were new concepts. Not only was this space going to be both, it was also to be preserved largely as wilderness. Our forested valley therefore represents a kind of monument to the value of wild woodlands in an urban setting.

> The trees of Rock Creek Park are Washington's living monument to the benefits of preserving a wilderness in the city.

Many trees in the Rock Creek Valley date back to the park's earliest days — and a few tall oaks may have started as acorns 250 years ago. Yet we continue to learn more about the benefits of having hundreds of wooded acres in the city. Trees improve the local climate, reduce air pollution, conserve water and support a wide diversity of plant and animal species. A forest can create a feeling of well-being and forge connections with nature not available along urban streets.

Forests of Change

Watch the trees and you can detect how Rock Creek Park changes from place to place, from season to season and over the decades.

Species usually found miles apart are just a short hike away because the park straddles the boundary between the Piedmont and Coastal Plain. Much of the woodlands are dominated by oaks, tulip trees and American beech. But descend to the flood plain and you will find sycamore, ash, pawpaw, cottonwood and other lowland species.

Spring bursts forth each year with the blooms of the redbud, dogwood, pawpaw, sassafras, tulip tree and American elm. Everywhere new leaves glow a golden green.

In summer, the mature canopy throws a veil over the forest floor. The leaves seem to capture all the sunlight, soaking in energy needed to produce nuts, fruits and berries of all shapes and hues. It is still just August when the tulip trees are first to drop their leaves. Soon patches of sky not visible since April begin to appear. Bright crimson breaks out on the leaves of the black gum, kicking off an autumn pageant of color that echoes through the forest.

Winter allows us to admire the variety within the park's barks. We observe distinctive textures. Peeling birches. The American hornbeam, whose sinewy and unyielding exterior earns it the nicknames of musclewood and ironwood. The Shingle Oak — once used, yes, to make shingles. We also see the colors of the trunks and branches standing out against the sky and snow, from the pewter of the American beech to the cinnamon brown of the river birch.

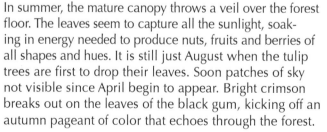

Rock Creek's lowland forest includes the Eastern cottonwood (left) and river birch (above), two trees with distinctive barks. The white-headed nuthatch (top) is commonly found nesting in natural cavities and hollows of park trees.

Branches of History

The primary forest that greeted English colonists was largely chopped down during the 18th and 19th centuries for logging, to clear land for farming and to provide an unobstructed view from the many Civil War fortifications. More trees fell when the park's borders were first defined, as property owners hurried to make money from timber on their land before having to hand the property over. Rock Creek commissioners went to court to outlaw tree cutting and hired two policemen to patrol the area.

Since the 1890 Rock Creek Park law called for "the preservation of all timber," most of the trees were then left undisturbed. However, official policy has not been totally hands-off. Early park authorities viewed with disdain the Virginia pine — at the time, one of the most common tree species. Their efforts to remove these native trees provoked President Woodrow Wilson to write a letter in 1920 complaining: "in one part of the park a whole plantation of young pines have been cut down and it made my heart ache to see it."

For ten years beginning in 1911, the US Forest Service planted thousands of non-native trees — including the California redwood — at an experimental plot on the north end of the park. The Service proposed to further develop the site as botanical gardens and a national arboretum. After that plan was rejected, more than 150 species of non-native trees were removed.

Other changes have altered the canopy. The red cedars that were quick to sprout in former farm fields were just as quick to die out — overwhelmed perhaps by the Japanese honeysuckle planted to reinforce the banks of park streams. Other invasives like English ivy similarly smother the trees. Non-native fungi and insect pests have endangered or wiped out various chestnut, beech, oak, hickory, hemlock and dogwood species.

New Dangers

Deer represent one of the biggest threats to today's trees. Due to over-population, the white-tailed does and bucks eat all the young trees as they sprout — preventing the forest from regenerating and threatening the food sources of native wildlife.

Climate change is another modern menace. Warmer temperatures favor some species while threatening others — and provide a more welcoming environment for destructive insects and diseases. As the calendar of seasonal change begins to shift, migratory birds may no longer find the proper food or shelter when they arrive. More extreme weather means more frequent droughts and storms.

Yet, despite all these challenges, the woodlands endure, wild and alive, bringing nature to the heart of Washington.

Two of the park's hairy woodpeckers tend to their young tucked away in a hole of a tree. The male arrives with a bill full of insects as the female flies off to find more.

Fall colors: National Park Service; Nuthatch and woodpeckers: Matthew Sileo/MatthewSileoPhotography.com; Sun through trees along Valley Trail: Lorraine Swerdloff; River birch, Eastern cottonwood, flowering cherry, towering Northern red oak: David Swerdloff.

U is for US Presidents

Before there ever was a Rock Creek Park, American Presidents were there grinding flour, enjoying picnics and getting shot at.

During a century of United States Presidents leading up to the establishment of the park in 1890, John Quincy Adams and Abraham Lincoln had the closest connections to Rock Creek Valley.

Just months before being elected, Adams purchased a gristmill along Rock Creek on property now part of the National Zoo. A year later, Adams concluded: "the business of the mill has been a losing concern … and instead of a resource for retirement is likely to prove a heavy clog upon my affairs." As predicted, he seldom made money from Adams' Mill, which he owned until his death in 1848.

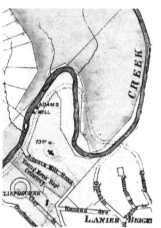

However, the wilderness did provide comfort, as biographer Charles Lanman wrote in 1856: "Many a time … did that distinguished statesman spend the morning under the dome of the capitol in debate, and the afternoon of the same day in this romantic glen, listening to the singing of the birds, which had built their nests in the branches of his own trees."

An 1887 real estate map (above) shows Adams Mill, as well as the road that bears its name. The mill also appears in an 1899 *Washington Post* engraving (upper left of the page).

The Rock (Creek) of Abraham

President Lincoln was a regular traveler into the wilderness just beyond the city. His family spent the warmer months at what we now call Lincoln's Cottage at the Soldiers' Home (which also served as a summer retreat for Presidents Hayes and Arthur). After the death of son Willie in 1862, the President sometimes crossed Rock Creek on trips from the cottage to the boy's grave in Georgetown.

Lincoln frequently visited soldiers at Civil War fortifications now under Rock Creek Park jurisdiction. One route from the White House took him through the valley along old Piney Branch Road. When Confederate forces threatened the capital at 1864's Battle of Fort Stevens, the President was at the fort during both days of fighting. On the second day, rebel sharpshooters wounded a Union surgeon standing just a few feet from Lincoln inside Fort Stevens — making Abe the only US President to come under enemy fire while in office. The same day, he also made history as the only commander-in-chief to issue a battlefield order, directing the shelling of private homes where Confederate marksmen had found cover.

"PRESIDENT LINCOLN WATCHING THE PROGRESS OF THE BATTLE."

Abraham Lincoln was nearly shot during the Battle of Fort Stevens on July 12, 1864. A newspaper engraving (above) portrays the President on the parapet of the fort. A plaque (below) dedicated in 1920 shows Lincoln standing near an Army surgeon who was wounded by a Confederate sharpshooter. Future Supreme Court Justice Oliver Wendell Holmes witnessed the scene and claimed he yelled out toward the President, "Get that damned fool down!"

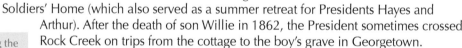
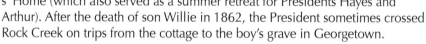

One of the generals commanding rebel troops during the battle was Kentucky's John Breckinridge, a former US Vice President and the cousin of Lincoln's wife Mary. He had also opposed Lincoln in the 1860 election, coming in second in the Electoral College.

More Executive Action

As a young man, James Madison traveled along the creek in 1769 on a journey from his Virginia home to study at Princeton. Historians cast doubt on accounts that President Franklin Pierce was arrested for running over a woman while driving his carriage along country roads near Rock Creek. Those who stick with the story say the charges were dropped but the incident made Pierce the first US President caught up in a criminal offense.

Meridian Hill Park (part of the Rock Creek system) features a statue of President James Buchanan. The memorial was funded from the estate of his niece, who served as White House hostess for her bachelor uncle. Because many lawmakers questioned whether Buchanan merited a memorial, it took Congress 15 years to accept the bequest.

As a repeat visitor to the Brightwood racetrack overlooking Rock Creek, President Grant was no stranger to the area. His grandson, Ulysses S. Grant III, would oversee the park from 1926 until shortly before the National Park Service assumed control in 1933. Grover Cleveland and his wife enjoyed carriage rides in the valley. During his first term, Cleveland signed the law creating the National Zoo along Rock Creek. He also donated a number of animals that went on exhibit there, including prairie dogs, mule deer, lynx and a golden eagle.

Andrew Johnson enjoyed picnicking near Peirce Mill. During his presidency, the Senate mandated a search for parkland where a new presidential mansion might be built. The report submitted in 1867 did not lead to a new White House. But it did promote Rock Creek Valley as worthy of a national park — a concept that became law in 1890 with the signature of President Benjamin Harrison.

Did Washington Sleep Here?

And what about the Father of Our Country? George Washington's bio is full of legends, and some may be true. Perhaps a young Washington did cross Rock Creek at Milkhouse Ford during the French and Indian War. Maybe he camped at the mouth of the creek in preparation for the ill-fated campaign by British Major General Edward Braddock to capture Fort Duquesne. Despite persistent claims that first surfaced in the 1870s, we do know that Georgetown's Old Stone House was never General Washington's headquarters during the American Revolution. Still, the structure (under Rock Creek Park supervision) dates back to 1765, making it DC's oldest building.

George Washington was supposed to be honored each summer in Rock Creek Park. Carter Barron Amphitheatre was constructed in 1950 in order to stage an annual pageant about his life. However, the musical *Faith of our Fathers* lasted just two seasons.

Mill engraving: *Washington Post* 8/18/1889; Souvenir program: George Washington University Libraries Special Collections; Ft. Stevens plaque: *National Tribune* 3/26/1903; Harrison signature: Wikimedia Commons; Lincoln plaque, Old Stone House (Carol M. Highsmith): Library of Congress; Hopkins Real Estate Atlas 1887: Washingtoniana Map Collection, DC Public Library; Buchanan statue: David Swerdloff; *Faith of Our Fathers* ad: *Evening Star* 9/23/1950, reprinted with permission of the DC Public Library, *Star* Collection, ©*Washington Post.*

For decades, the Old Stone House on M Street (above left) was mistakenly credited as George Washington's headquarters during the Revolutionary War. A 1950 newspaper ad (above) promotes a historic pageant about President Washington staged at Rock Creek Park's Carter Barron Amphitheatre (see souvenir program on previous page). The venue was originally called the Sesquicentennial Amphitheatre to commemorate the 150th anniversary of Washington, DC as the nation's capital.

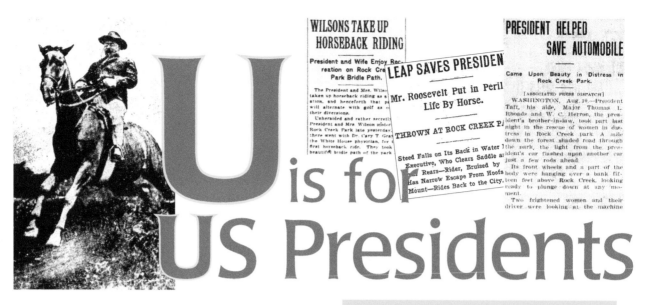

U is for US Presidents

T heodore Roosevelt wrote about the park in his auto- biography: "When our children were little … each Sunday afternoon the whole family spent in Rock Creek Park, which was then very real country indeed."

Both Roosevelts made Rock Creek history — while for other 20th century Presidents, the park was a place for courting, golfing, riding and politicking.

He also led frequent hikes with friends and soldiers: "Often … we would arrange for a point to point walk, not turning aside for anything…. We like Rock Creek for these walks because we could do so much scrambling and climbing along the cliffs." One of his regular companions was French ambassador Jean Jules Jusserand, who was honored with his own memorial in 1936.

THEODORE ROOSEVELT
SIDE TRAIL
BEACH DRIVE AND
BLAGDEN AVE. 0.2 MI

Teddy is often credited with naming Boulder Bridge. After losing a gold ring on an outing in 1902, the President placed a "Lost and Found" ad claiming the ring went missing "100 yards above boulder bridge." Today's park visitors hike nearby along the Theodore Roosevelt side trail.

Other stories about TR focus on his adventures skinny- dipping in Rock Creek and riding horses through the park. The President took a nasty fall in 1908 when his mount became frightened on the Broad Branch ford. Jumping from the saddle, he landed in the water "completely clear of the horse, and to that circumstance he probably owes his life." (*Washington Post*, 6/4/1908).

Sometimes Teddy was accompanied by his Secretary of War (and future President) William Howard Taft. Taft took delight in the Rock Creek wilderness, making frequent jaunts into the park during his long Washington career. The Connecticut Avenue Bridge was renamed in his honor in 1931. "Taft was a keen admirer of the structure," the *Evening Star* reported (4/9/1931). "He was often seen crossing it on foot in the course of his rambles about the Rock Creek Valley."

Theodore Roosevelt leading 50 Army officers on a trek through Rock Creek Park in 1908. The *Baltimore Sun* article describes TR wading waist-deep in the creek and tearing through brambles before conquering a 60-foot bluff: "Catch- ing at root and rock, the President went at the face of the cliff, and the chimpanzee in the Zoo across the park instinctively felt that some- body was going him one better."

The Park Gets a New Deal

Initiatives by President Franklin D. Roosevelt during the 1930s created much of the park infrastructure we see today through New Deal agencies such as the Civilian Conservation Corps, Works Progress Administration and Public Works Administration. Unemployed Americans were put to work building footbridges, paths and horse trails; erecting the Park Police station and other buildings; planting trees and shrubs; renovating Peirce Mill, Klingle Mansion and Fort Stevens; and helping to construct Piney Branch Parkway.

Beginning in 1941, FDR would also tour Rock Creek by car with his long-time paramour Lucy Mercer Rutherfurd — but only when Eleanor was out of town.

Wooing and Zooing

Woodrow Wilson enjoyed walks and drives in the park, where he courted his second wife Edith in 1915. The chauffeur would drop them off along Ross Drive and the pair would stroll together through the woods. Shortly after leaving office in 1921, Wilson wrote a letter protesting the construction of the Rock Creek Golf Course. Nevertheless, President Warren Harding would inaugurate the course in 1923, shooting 102. Three decades later, the White House was occupied by avid golfer Dwight Eisenhower, who was known to tee off at the links in Rock Creek Park.

The Coolidge family was so fond of animals that their White House was sometimes called the Pennsylvania Avenue Zoo. Many of the creatures ended up along Rock Creek at the National Zoo, including a black bear, lion cubs and a hippo. The Coolidges also adopted a pet raccoon they named Rebecca — saving her from becoming part of a Thanksgiving meal. She was sent to the zoo after several escapes from the White House grounds.

Herbert Hoover lived up to the nickname "The Great Engineer" during park visits. On family picnics by the creek, he would recruit volunteers to help him construct miniature dams.

President Harry Truman attended the opening of the DC Sesquicentennial Amphitheatre in 1950, and returned in 1951 when it was dedicated to the late Carter Barron. Truman would also purchase flour and meal from Peirce Mill for use in the White House.

Civilian Conservation Corpsmen (above) work on the ornamental dam at Peirce Mill in 1936.

FDR, Eleanor Roosevelt and Mme. Jusserand arrive in the park (right) for the unveiling of a memorial to Jean Jules Jusserand, also in 1936.

President Truman at Rock Creek's outdoor amphitheatre in 1951 for its dedication to the late Carter Barron.

Though Jimmy Carter is said to have jogged in Rock Creek valley, he was so new to the nation's capital when he took office in 1977 that members of the press corps joked "President Carter knows so little about Washington he thinks Rock Creek Park is a Korean lobbyist."

Ronald Reagan occasionally rode horses on park trails and practiced horse jumping at the Equitation Field. When he was first elected, several Secret Service agents received expedited training in Rock Creek Park so they could protect him on horseback. Not all of the agents attained a suitable level of horsemanship.

Some of Bill Clinton's jogging trips took him into the park, where he would stop to shake hands and sign autographs. To promote Clean Water legislation in 1995, President Clinton used Peirce Mill as a backdrop, pointing out signs by the creek that warned of poisons and pollutants: "To those who say we have nothing more to do to clean up America's waterways, I urge them to come here to Peirce Mill and read the sign. We still have a lot of work to do on this, the most simple necessity of our lives, water."

President Barack Obama also went politicking within the Rock Creek system, promoting his highway plan in 2014 with a speech at Georgetown Waterfront Park.

Newspaper images at top of previous page (L to R): *Evening Star* 5/26/1907, *Washington Times* 4/26/1917, *Washington Post* 6/4/1908, *Arizona Republican* 8/11/1912; "The President in the Woods" (TR rock climbing, 1908) and FDR at Jusserand memorial (11/7/1936): Library of Congress; "Led 50 on Wild Walk": *Baltimore Sun* 11/8/1908; Trail sign: David Swerdloff; CCC crew (1936): National Park Service; Truman at dedication of Carter Barron Amphitheatre: National Archives.

V is for Volunteers

Volunteers arrive in Rock Creek Valley every week carrying axes and garden gloves, working with ponies and pandas, advancing public knowledge and scientific research. They represent the National Park Service and more than a dozen organizations working to preserve and protect the resources along Rock Creek and associated park areas.

Some volunteer opportunities are within the NPS itself — for example, helping out at the Nature Center and summer camps. The Park Service (as well as Montgomery Parks) also provides training to help certify volunteers to properly remove invasive plants from parkland. But there are many other ways to donate your time.

Volunteer Path-ologists

If a tree falls in the forest — whether anyone hears it or not — the Potomac Appalachian Trail Club will hear about it should the downed tree block a trail. For decades PATC volunteers have worked with park rangers to maintain Rock Creek Park's hiking and horse trails, without using power tools. They invite the public to join them on work trips a couple of times a month, usually on Saturday mornings. Don't worry: they'll train you to use axes, handsaws and other traditional tools safely and effectively.

> Without volunteers, the park would be overrun with vines, trails would be blocked and eroded, and many public programs would come to a halt.

Potomac Appalachian Trail Club volunteers (above and top) clear and shore up Rock Creek Park trails.

PATC volunteers build the "cribbing" that keeps trails from collapsing into waterways. They construct steps to get hikers up slopes and arrange stones to help them hop across streams. And they erase so-called "social trails" — unofficial paths created by people (and dogs) that fragment wildlife habitats and are poorly located within the park landscape.

Supporting All of the Park

Rock Creek Conservancy is the only NPS partner dedicated solely to Rock Creek and its parks. Its mission is to revitalize the entire watershed for present and future generations — from the creek's headwaters in Montgomery County through Rock Creek Park in DC to the outflow at the Potomac River.

Young Rock Creek Conservancy volunteers remove trash from the creek during the 2011 Extreme Cleanup.

Neighborhoods volunteer to adopt a section of the creek and its tributaries as one of the Conservancy's Stream Teams. Dozens of citizen squads monitor "their" piece of Rock Creek and organize clean-up days. RCC sponsors two parkwide efforts each year. In the first seven years of the Rock Creek Extreme Cleanup — held each April since 2009 — volunteers removed more than 70 tons of junk and 16,000 bags of trash along the creek in DC and Maryland. RCC also recruits Rock Creek Ambassadors to educate the public and advocacy volunteers to attend public meetings, write letters and encourage support for Rock Creek Park.

DC's last remaining grist mill along Rock Creek is once again grinding flour, thanks to activism and fundraising by the volunteers of Friends of Pierce Mill. The group also offers opportunities to serve as interpreters at the mill, to help maintain the fruit trees planted to commemorate the Peirce family orchards and to lead education and children's programs.

Other parks within the Rock Creek system have their own conservancies and friends groups. Among them is Dumbarton Oaks Park Conservancy, which aims not only to preserve and beautify, but also to renew the 1921 vision of landscape designer Beatrix Farrand in what is her last remaining wild garden.

Special Interest Groups

Whatever your special interest, there's a volunteer program that will appeal to you.

The Rock Creek Horse Center needs folks to lead public trail rides, groom and clean up after the horses, and help out at summer camps.

A Rock Creek Horse Center volunteer grooms a horse before a public trail ride. Below, a FONZ volunteer operates the Panda Cam, looking for unusual behaviors as animal lovers observe online.

Amateur historians support the Civil War sites overseen by Rock Creek Park — from Fort DeRussy east to Fort Bunker Hill — through programs organized by the NPS and groups like the Alliance to Preserve the Civil War Defenses of Washington. Volunteers interpret and even re-enact events more than 150 years ago that saved the nation's capital.

Volunteers from the DC Audubon Society conduct birdwatching field trips into the park and support the Rock Creek Songbirds Project, which has planted hundreds of native trees and shrubs crucial to the park's dwindling population of songbirds.

Many environmental programs benefit from volunteers from the non-profit Casey Trees, which also recruits citizen scientists to monitor seasonal changes in the valley's tree canopy.

More Creekside Collaborations

FONZ — Friends of the National Zoo — provides tens of thousands of hours of service each year supporting threatened species housed along Rock Creek. Animal interpreters, zoo guides and camp aides deal with the public. Keeper aides get down and dirty with the animals. Behavior Watchers gather research data, and some operate the zoo's famous Panda Cam.

Members of National Capital Astronomers co-sponsor the park's monthly Exploring the Sky programs under the stars. Special events also depend on volunteers — from tennis scorekeepers and ballpersons at the Citi Open to birders participating in the Christmas Bird Count.

Despite the many challenges that threaten the land, water and historic structures within Rock Creek Park, funding levels are under increasing pressure. Volunteers working on behalf of the park and its many partners remain a crucial factor in any plan for a bright future for Washington's urban oasis.

PATC photos courtesy Potomac Appalachian Trail Club Rock Creek Crew; Extreme Cleanup photo: Rock Creek Conservancy; Horse Center and FONZ photos: David Swerdloff.

W is for Who What When Where Why?

Test your knowledge of Rock Creek Park by answering 30 questions that begin with the five **W**s

It's time to separate the Rock Creek Rookies from the Park Prodigies. Your exam is part trivia, part history, part nature — and all in fun.

The answers are on the following pages. Good luck!

Who?

1. Who were the contrabands?
2. Who were six Rock Creek Valley property owners who have roads in or near the park named after them?
3. Who were the demonstrators (right) who walked through Rock Creek Valley on the first "march on Washington"?
4. Who was the Whitehurst Woman?
5. Who wrote: "We would arrange for a point to point walk, not turning aside for anything…. On several occasions we thus swam Rock Creek … when the ice was floating thick upon it"?
6. Who did the House of Representatives vote to name Rock Creek Park after — in 1890?
7. Who was the TV western star who, early in his career, played New York Gov. George Clinton in a historic pageant in Rock Creek Park?

What?

8. What activity was prohibited in Rock Creek Park beginning in the summer of 1936?
9. What two National Parks were authorized before Rock Creek Park?
10. What does the inscription on Peirce Mill "BIP 1829" stand for?
11. What are the two stone structures along Rock Creek and Potomac Parkway just north of the K Street overpass?
12. What tributary of Rock Creek has resumed its natural flow after being coursed through a pipe since the 1930s?
13. What 1993 movie has a scene set at a West Virginia cabin but filmed in Rock Creek Park?
14. What three wild species related to dogs can be found living in Rock Creek Park?
15. What kind of living things are the lichen (left) we commonly find on park rocks?
16. What piece of the Rock Creek Park system was completed in 2011 along the Potomac River?
17. What word fills in the blank of this 1922 *Washington Post* report on a nighttime parking ban within the park: "It is manifestly unfair to penalize all the people because the park authorities are unable to cope with the _____ situation in Rock Creek Park"?

When?

18. When did Rock Creek Park become part of the National Park Service?

19. When did the NPS set aside one lane of Rock Creek and Potomac Parkway for bicycle commuters?

Where?

20. Where is the landmark that completes this 1864 *Evening Star* report: "The hills, trees and fences within sight of _____ were covered with human beings quite a number of whom were ladies"?

21. Where is the home country of the first champion of a pro tennis tournament on Rock Creek courts (in 1969)?

22. Where did Smokey Robinson perform his final concerts with the Miracles?

23. Where was the park's first Nature Center (left) located (beginning in October 1956)?

24. Where in the Rock Creek Park system can you conduct wedding ceremonies by special permit?

Why?

25. Why did a powerful searchlight sweep the night sky from Rock Creek Park November 6, 1928?

26. Why do most alphabetical streets west of the park (e.g. Albemarle, Brandywine, Chesapeake…) have different names than those east of the park (Allison, Buchanan, Crittenden…)?

27. Why did the reconstruction of the Wilson Bridge improve the ecology of Rock Creek?

28. Why is a stone (left) — located about 100 feet from the northernmost point of Rock Creek Park — considered significant?

29. Why are local naturalists so interested in a tiny shrimp-like invertebrate (right) known as the Hay's spring amphipod?

30. Why are dog owners required to keep their pets on-leash within the park?

Answers

▼

Answers

WHO

1. The word contraband referred to **African American slaves who fled the Confederacy and were put to work by the Union army**. A large group of contrabands was based at Camp Brightwood (left), just south of Fort Stevens. Many of these workers helped build the fortifications around Washington, DC, often at little or no pay. The first contrabands were classified as property, essentially "contraband of war" that would not be returned since their labor would have aided the rebel cause. Federal policy declared contrabands to be free in August 1861.

2. The Peirces: Peirce Mill Road (off Park Road); **the Klingles:** Klingle Road; **the Shoemakers:** Shoemaker Street (off Tilden Street); **Thomas Blagden:** Blagden Avenue and Terrace; **John Quincy Adams:** Adams Mill Road; dairymen **George & Joseph Wise:** Wise Road. Daniels Road (now Oregon Avenue), Moreland Road (Utah Avenue) and Swart Road (27th Street) had also been named after local property owners.

3. Coxey's Army was a group of unemployed workers demanding public works programs in response to the economic depression of the 1890s. Their unlikely leader was rich businessman Jacob Coxey. In 1894 they walked from Ohio to the Capitol, holding their final camp near the park's present-day recreation area along 16th Street — then marching into town through Rock Creek Valley along the old Piney Branch Road.

4. Whitehurst Woman is the name given to the Native American whose cremated remains were found (along with a number of American Indian artifacts) about 250 feet east of Rock Creek near the Whitehurst Freeway. She may represent the first wave of Algonquians into the area some 1,300 years ago.

5. Theodore Roosevelt led family, friends and associates on rambles to a distant point — testing his companions on their ability to go "over or through, never around."

6. With the 400th anniversary of Columbus' first voyage to America just two years away, the House voted to call the new public land "**Columbus Memorial Park.**" In conference committee, the Senate's preference of Rock Creek Park won out, but the law retained a House mandate that half the cost of purchasing land for the park be borne by DC.

7. Pernell Roberts, the future Adam Cartwright on *Bonanza*, appeared in the historic pageant *Faith of Our Fathers*.

WHAT

8. Car washing

9. Yellowstone (1872) **and Sequoia** (established two days before Rock Creek Park in 1890). Yosemite — set aside by Congress for preservation in 1864 but ceded to California as a state park — was named a national park four days after RCP. Congress gave federal protection to Hot Springs Reservation in 1832, but didn't make it a national park until 1921. Mackinac National Park was established in 1875 but decommissioned in 1895.

10. Either "**Built by Isaac Peirce**" or "**Betsy and Isaac Peirce,**" plus the year the mill was finished.

11. They are all that remain of **Godey's Lime Kilns** (shown on next page), which melted limestone brought downstream along the C & O Canal. The original four ovens — in use from 1833 to 1908 — mainly produced "quicklime" used to seal masonry.

12. The **Broad Branch stream** (above) was "daylighted" in 2014.

13. *The Pelican Brief.* The scene was shot in the narrow strip of the park near 18th and Shepherd Streets in Crestwood.

14. Red foxes, gray foxes and **coyotes**

15. Lichens represent a combination of at least two types of living things. What we see are **fungi**. However, they collect moisture and provide shelter for **algae** and/or **cyanobacteria,** allowing them to grow in inhospitable conditions like the surface of a rock. Through photosynthesis, the other organisms supply nutrients for the fungi.

16. Georgetown Waterfront Park

17. Spooning (clipping below)

SCORE PARKING EDICT

Citizens Roused at Night Auto Ban in Rock Creek Park.

DEMAND RULING BE REVOKED

Condemn It as Ill-Advised Attack on Liberties of the People.

Unfair to Penalize All Because of Offenses by Few, Declare Indignant Civic Leaders—Call Order Futile and a Species of Military Oppression—Believe It Unnecessary if Authorities Enforce Law.

Efforts are being made by citizens to have Lieut. Col. C. O. Sherrill, superintendent of public buildings and grounds, rescind his recent order, effective July 24, prohibiting parking at night in Rock Creek park. The cry of protest against the edict is growing in volume, and citizens all over the city, including those who do not own automobiles, are denouncing the order as "another foolish and ill-advised regulation attacking the liberties of the people."

Those opposed to the order declare that it is manifestly unfair to penalize all the people because the park authorities are unable to cope with the "spooning" situation in Rock

WHEN

18. Although the National Park Service was established in 1916, Rock Creek Park was not added to the system until **August 10, 1933**. At that time, the service was called the Office of National Parks, Buildings and Reservations. So, technically, RCP was not part of the NPS until the National Park Service name was restored March 2, 1934.

19. In **1971**, the park service tried reserving one lane of the parkway for bicycle commuters. The experiment lasted just a week after drivers complained about traffic jams. Bicyclists did receive one lasting benefit: the NPS paved the equestrian trail from Connecticut Avenue south to Virginia Avenue as a biking/hiking path.

20. Fort Stevens. Spectators who traveled from the city for an outing instead witnessed killing and chaos. The battlefield was strewn with bodies of the dead and dying. Nearby homes were destroyed and others were burned by Union troops to take cover away from retreating Confederate soldiers.

21. Brazil. Thomaz Koch defeated Arthur Ashe in five sets in the final of the first Washington Star International.

22. Carter Barron Amphitheatre. Highlights from the three performances July 14-16, 1972 were released later that year as the double album *Smokey Robinson and The Miracles 1957-1972* (also part of the 2004 Miracles CD set, *The Live! Collection*).

23. Inside the **Klingle Mansion**.

24. Meridian Hill Park, **Montrose Park**, and the **garden of the Old Stone House**.

WHY

25. The 300-million-candlepower searchlight (and a twin at the District Building) gave DC residents **presidential election results**. If Al Smith was in the lead, the lights burned continuously. If they flashed on and off, Herbert Hoover was ahead. A pilot also flew over the area firing red or green flares to indicate the leader.

W. H. Godey advertises products from his lime kilns, 1856 (right). An early 20th century photo of the kiln ruins (top) suggests the scale of the operation. The ruins in 2008 (above).

LIME!—LIME!!—LIME!!! — WILL BE OPENED TO-MORROW, AT the Lime Kilns of W. H. Godey & Co., situated on Rock Creek, between the upper and lower bridges, a kiln of very superior WOOD BURNT LIME. The subscribers have also on hand a large supply of PLASTERERS' HAIR, CEMENT, CALCINED PLASTER, and every description of the very best quality of lime, which will be disposed of on the most reasonable terms. ap 14—cotf — W. H. GODEY & CO.

26. On August 14, 1901, the Washington, DC Commissioners announced a plan for naming streets in more than 100 subdivisions, mainly east of the park. East-west streets would continue to be arranged in alphabetical order — **but they had to be named after famous Americans**. So familiar names west of the park — like Albemarle and Brandywine — were not used in the new developments.

27. To mitigate damage done to other streams by Wilson Bridge construction, the project **removed barriers in Rock Creek that prevented fish from swimming upstream to spawn**. The most ambitious measure involved building a fish ladder around the Peirce Mill dam.

28. It is DC's northernmost **Boundary Stone** (right), marking the tip of the diamond shape that formed the original District. Sometimes called the oldest federal monuments, 40 stones were inscribed and put in place in 1791 and 1792.

29. The Hay's spring amphipod is believed to be the **only endangered species living in the park** — and the park is its only home.

30. Dogs that venture off trails trample and erode wild areas, fragmenting habitat and taking "safe zones" away from wildlife. Their fur can spread the seeds of invasive plants. Even the friendliest dog can appear to be a threat to park visitors (and some dogs truly are). Keeping dogs on-leash allows owners to control interactions with other dogs and wild animals. Dogs that play in the water are at risk from bacteria and chemical pollutants in the creek.

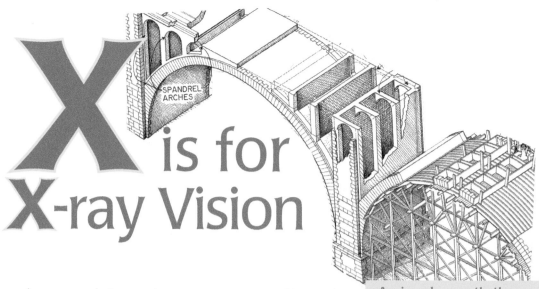

X is for X-ray Vision

SPANDREL ARCHES

Super heroes can do it — and now you can, too: use X-ray vision to learn more about what's around you in Rock Creek Park.

Peer through the walls of a 19th century mill to observe how the creek powers a marvelous array of elevators, augers and millstones. Use your new superpower to see that the boulders of Boulder Bridge are only a facade and the graceful arches of the Taft Bridge are made of simple concrete poured into forms. Look underwater at a fish ladder that provides a path around a waterfall. And discern the forest's natural cycle in which trees take in carbon, nitrogen and other elements and return them into the environment.

A view beneath the surface shows the magnificent complexity of what we see in Rock Creek Park.

Hardly Run-of-the-Mill

Peirce Mill embodies what had been revolutionary advances in the milling industry. In constructing the mill in the 1820s, the Peirce family incorporated innovative designs and labor-saving devices first described in 1795 by Delaware miller Oliver Evans.

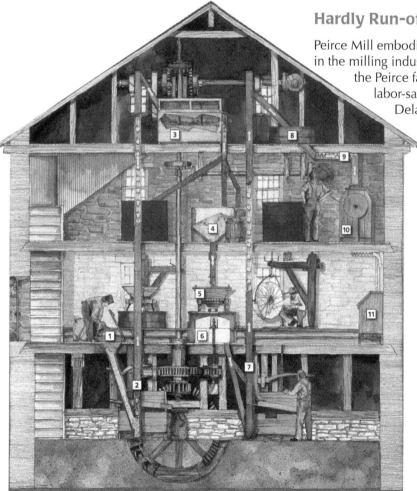

The cutaway view (left) shows how grain loaded into the receiving hopper (1) falls to the basement, where an elevator (2) lifts it to the top floor. A rolling screen (3) separates out foreign objects and deposits the grain into a storage bin (4). When it is ready for milling, the grain drops into a hopper (5) which releases a regulated flow of grain onto the lower millstone, called the bedstone (6). The top stone, called the runner stone, rotates at about 125 revolutions per minute a fraction of an inch above the bedstone, cutting the grain to produce a warm, moist meal. The meal falls down a chute to the basement where another elevator (7) lifts it to a hopper (8) on the top floor to cool and dry. An auger (9) continues the drying process and advances the meal to the bolter (10). Fine and medium mesh screens in the bolter separate the meal into flour, middlings and bran that are stored in separate holding bins (11).

During the 19th century, Rock Creek flowed higher and faster than it does today, powering numerous mills conveniently located just a wagon ride away from the port of Georgetown. Water from the stream, channeled through a trough called a millrace, turned the wooden waterwheel outside each mill — which, linked by gears and belts, powered the movement inside. Peirce Mill has employed two different wheel configurations: an overshot wheel and a breast wheel. Water pours onto an overshot wheel just past the wheel's highest point, while the current strikes a breast wheel at about axle height.

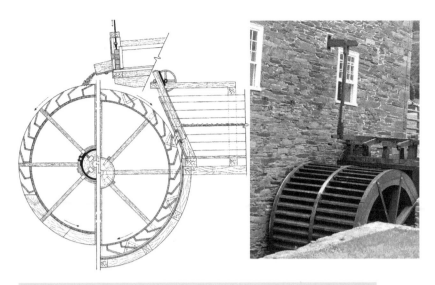

An overshot mill wheel and a breast mill wheel turn in opposite directions. The overshot wheel in the left half of the drawing revolves counter-clockwise. The breast wheel in the right half turns clockwise. Peirce Mill's current water wheel is pictured at right.

Boulders of Beauty

Boulder Bridge serves as one of the enduring symbols of Rock Creek Park. Its huge stones — some of them weighing more than half a ton — were carefully selected to harmonize with the rocks in the creek and on the hillsides. But they are only decoration, attached by wrought iron "cramps" to the steel girders that support the span (inset below).

The builders had to pay a royalty to use the Melan method of construction, patented just nine years before the bridge was completed in 1902. Under this process, a series of steel lattice arches (seen in the cutaway below) was arranged side by side across the creek, supported by concrete abutments on each bank. Then the girders themselves were encased in concrete.

Boulder Bridge was built under the direction of Lansing Beach of the US Army Corps of Engineers, who served as Rock Creek Park supervisor and DC engineer commissioner. He also supervised the construction of Rock Creek Drive, which was renamed Beach Driveway — and then Beach Drive — in his honor.

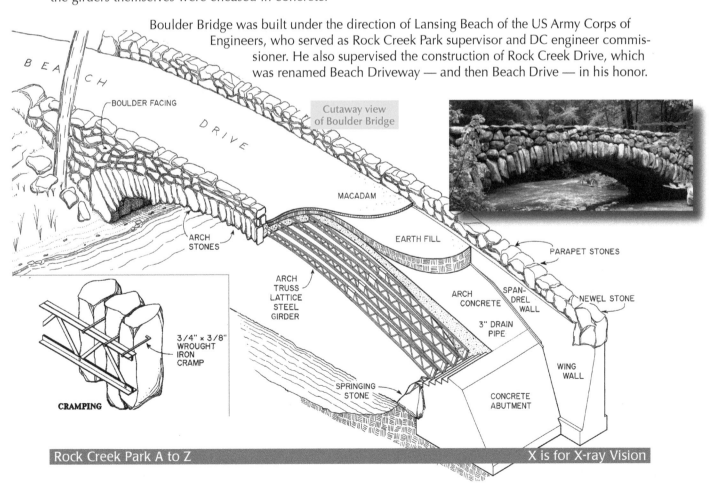

BEACH

BOULDER FACING

DRIVE

Cutaway view of Boulder Bridge

MACADAM

EARTH FILL

ARCH STONES

ARCH TRUSS LATTICE STEEL GIRDER

PARAPET STONES

ARCH CONCRETE

SPAN-DREL WALL

NEWEL STONE

3" DRAIN PIPE

3/4" x 3/8" WROUGHT IRON CRAMP

WING WALL

CRAMPING

SPRINGING STONE

CONCRETE ABUTMENT

Tree-cology

When nature is in balance, the forest is part of a grand cycle. Carbon, nitrogen, calcium and other key nutrients are transferred from the trees to the soil to the air and then back to the trees through processes such as uptake, respiration and decomposition. During photosynthesis, the leaves use energy from sunlight to make food (glucose) from carbon dioxide and water in a reaction that also releases oxygen into the air.

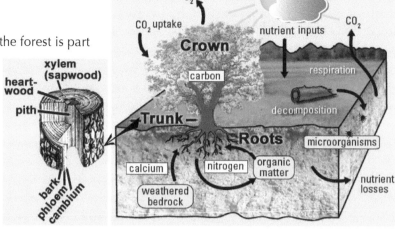

Within the trunk of a tree, each layer has a function. The bark protects the tree. Food made in the leaves flows down through the phloem to be stored or used in the cambium to create a new ring of sapwood (xylem) each year. The xylem draws water and nutrients up from the roots. The inactive cells of the heartwood provide stability and surround the narrow channel called the pith.

Bypass along Herring Highway

Until a fish ladder was completed in 2006, the dam and ornamental waterfall near Peirce Mill blocked the path of migrating fish. The fishway now allows species like blueback herring, alewife and striped bass to swim around the waterfall to reach ancestral spawning habitats upstream.

Their route from the Potomac River to upper Rock Creek has been dubbed Herring Highway. At one time, streams like Rock Creek teemed with fish during their spring migration. As historian Robert Beverly wrote in 1705, "Herrings come up in such abundance into their brooks and fords that it is almost impossible to ride through without treading on them."

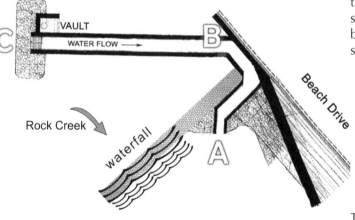

The fish ladder (viewed from above) gives migrating fish a navigable route upstream around the 1905 dam and waterfall by Peirce Mill.

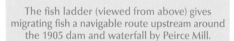

The view from above (left) shows how fish bypass the waterfall by entering at A and swimming "uphill" from B to C. As water pours into the fishway at C, baffles installed in slots between B and C regulate the current. They also provide resting spots for fish between the baffles. The side view (below) shows the placement of the baffles, with an inset drawing of how they would appear from C.

Researchers can climb down into the "vault" and look through a window at fish exiting the ladder.

Side view of the fish ladder (below) shows the window in the "vault" and the placement of the baffles. Fish can rest between the baffles (inset), which also control the velocity of the water.

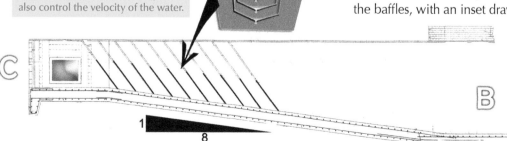

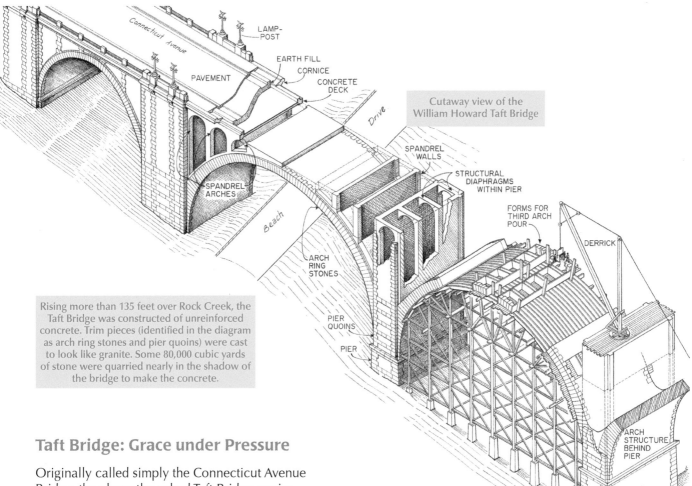

LAMP-POST

Connecticut Avenue

EARTH FILL
CORNICE

PAVEMENT

CONCRETE DECK

Drive

Cutaway view of the
William Howard Taft Bridge

SPANDREL WALLS

STRUCTURAL DIAPHRAGMS WITHIN PIER

SPANDREL ARCHES

FORMS FOR THIRD ARCH POUR

DERRICK

Beach

ARCH RING STONES

PIER QUOINS

PIER

ARCH STRUCTURE BEHIND PIER

Rising more than 135 feet over Rock Creek, the Taft Bridge was constructed of unreinforced concrete. Trim pieces (identified in the diagram as arch ring stones and pier quoins) were cast to look like granite. Some 80,000 cubic yards of stone were quarried nearly in the shadow of the bridge to make the concrete.

Taft Bridge: Grace under Pressure

Originally called simply the Connecticut Avenue Bridge, the elegantly arched Taft Bridge carries Connecticut Avenue high over Rock Creek Valley. When it was finished in 1907, it was said to be the largest unreinforced concrete structure in the world. The popular term for the new span was the Million Dollar Bridge, though that overstated its cost by about 18 percent. It was renamed for President William Howard Taft in 1931.

Arches are able to support weight because the stones in an arch press against each other, creating an upward force equivalent to the downward pull of gravity. Multiple arches also buttress one another, adding extra support and allowing the piers between them to be smaller.

Instead of stone, the seven graceful arches of the Taft Bridge are made of unreinforced concrete. In the drawing (above), workers near the derrick are pouring concrete into a form close to the crown of one of the arches.

Each pier is comprised of four "diaphragms" for added strength. While most of the arches have a span of 150 feet, the ones on each end only span 82 feet. That results in a greater load on the end piers, which had to be nearly twice as wide as the others.

Mill drawing, fish ladder diagrams: National Park Service (adapted by David and Lorraine Swerdloff); Mill wheel, Boulder Bridge and Taft Bridge diagrams: Library of Congress (adapted); Mill wheel, Boulder Bridge and tree photos: David Swerdloff; Forest ecology diagram: USGS (adapted); Tree trunk diagram: Catalonia Educational Telematic Network through Wikimedia Commons (adapted); Taft Bridge photo, 2007: Scott S through Flickr.com under Creative Commons 2.0 license, cropped.

Y is for You Gotta Be Kidding!

· PROPOSED ·
· EXECVTIVE MANSION ·

In an alternate universe, a visitor to Rock Creek Park might: go boating on the lake between Woodley Park and Military Road; drive along the Aspen Street overpass for a view of the Botanic Garden; visit every one of the park's 50 state museums; tour the handsome mansions on land reclaimed by channeling Rock Creek through an underground culvert; or head out of town on an expressway where Beach Drive is today.

Your reaction may be, "You gotta be kidding!" But the history of the park includes serious proposals that would have made all of that — and more — possible.

They wanted to do *what* to Rock Creek Valley? Flood it, fill it in, pave it, load it with monuments? YGBK!

Rock Creek Lake

An 1883 plan to dam Rock Creek may have resulted in this artificial lake. Displayed in blue is all land at an altitude below 150 feet, the height of the proposed dam.

As civic leaders were promoting the establishment of Rock Creek Park during the 1880s, the DC official in charge of the city's water and sewage systems had a competing vision. Captain Richard Hoxie wanted the centerpiece of the park to be a reservoir four miles long. This artificial lake would be created by constructing a masonry dam 150 feet high above Georgetown. Hoxie estimated that about 1,300 acres would be flooded, but he considered nearly the entire expanse "worthless for any other purpose, being precipitous, rocky hillside, covered with thickets of laurel and small timber."

High Bridges and Fast Roads

In the first comprehensive plan for the park, Olmsted Brothers recommended a pair of tall bridges over Rock Creek. Their 1918 report called for these "high-level viaduct type" routes to carry cross-town traffic above the park instead of relying on at-grade crossings. By 1930, planning maps from the National Capital Park and Planning Commission had increased the number of spans to three. The northern bridge would have extended Aspen Street west to Western Avenue. The middle one would have taken Madison and Kennedy Streets west to Utah Avenue, so that Military Road remained an at-grade link with the park. The lower span was to bring Taylor and Upshur Streets west to both Linnean Avenue and a new road roughly following today's Melvin Hazen trail. Even as late as 1959, planning officials were endorsing a six-lane "Cross-Park Freeway" to be built above Melvin Hazen Park that connected Tenley Circle with a proposed "inner loop" freeway at T Street.

Cross-Park Freeway Project Wins Support

Maryland Planners Ask For Rock Creek Route

Tenley Circle To T Street Plan Backed

Map shows an 1886 plan to channel part of Rock Creek underground. 1959 news articles describe proposals for a freeway across the park from Tenley Circle and an expressway up Rock Creek to connect with the future I-270. In an article that appeared alongside the latter story, a US Senator from Maryland complains about delays in building a highway up Glover-Archbold Park.

Highway planners also looked north and south, dreaming for decades about constructing an expressway along Rock Creek. The first major push came after Rock Creek and Potomac Parkway was completed in 1936. Through the years, the proposals ranged from simply extending the parkway to using the right-of-way along the creek to build a high-speed route to what eventually became I-270. The fact that no highway was built is both a tribute to preservationists and to the difficulty of reaching an agreement among all the stakeholders — including DC and Maryland planners, the National Park Service, federal highway officials and the National Zoo.

Put It in a Pipe

Another perennial proposal was to place part of lower Rock Creek into an underground channel, creating new development possibilities on the property above. DC officials fended off one of the earliest attempts in 1892. A Senate resolution instructed them to develop a plan to submerge the creek south of Massachusetts Avenue and estimate the value of the filled land. City engineers argued that debris could clog the underground channel, causing a back-up that might flood large parts of the District.

Three "High Level Crossings" of Rock Creek Park appear on a 1930 plan from the National Capital Park and Planning Commission.

Even in the 20th century, one of the leading alternatives for Rock Creek and Potomac Parkway was the so-called "closed-valley plan" in which much of the lower creek would be channeled into a conduit. The valley above would have been filled in to create a boulevard lined with stately homes.

CONGRESS URGED TO PLACE LINCOLN MEMORIAL ON MERIDIAN HILL

The Lincoln Memorial Commission rejected John Russell Pope's 1912 design (above, top) and its location on Meridian Hill. The other design shown, by F. V. Murphy and W.B. Olmsted, placed Lincoln in a grand arch on Meridian Hill. At the top of the preceding page is an 1898 plan by Paul Pelz for a new presidential mansion on the site.

Gardens and Museums

The Rock Creek Park system includes nearly two dozen monuments and memorials, including one within the actual park boundaries (the Jusserand Memorial honoring a longtime French ambassador). However, the park could have been crowded with monuments. A House bill in 1898 proposed building a series of "state exhibition buildings" in Rock Creek Park — essentially museums for each of the states. For more than 20 years thereafter, attempts were made to authorize such buildings somewhere in the DC area.

The United States Botanic Garden had a number of homes before moving to its present location near the US Capitol. To some influential lawmakers, Rock Creek Park seemed to be the perfect spot. Effective opposing voices came from the Commission of Fine Arts and from Olmsted Brothers, who argued in 1918 that "the inevitable result" would be "the gradual frittering away of a priceless and self-consistent piece of natural scenery."

The rest of the Rock Creek system was not immune to dubious schemes. For more than 40 years (until 1967), DC transportation plans called for a highway up Glover-Archbold Park. Various edifices were proposed for Meridian Hill, including a new presidential mansion, the Lincoln Memorial and a grand Lincoln arch to anchor a highway originating in Gettysburg.

These plans — and others — may seem so foolhardy today we can only give thanks they never were approved. But one project that did get built overlooking Rock Creek is guaranteed to inspire cries of "You gotta be kidding!"

Unlike today — when deer are overrunning the park — back in 1874 they had long been exterminated from the area. That's when Thomas Blagden decided to import some deer from the Adirondacks, breed them on 20 or 30 acres of his land on the east bank of Rock Creek, and sell the offspring to estate owners for their personal game parks. Washingtonians would travel up Piney Branch Road just to peer through the fence of the Blagden Deer Park to try to get a glimpse. Deer as exotic animals? Not kidding!

In a 1904 letter from the White House to his son Archie, President Theodore Roosevelt drew a picture of a fawn he startled after he "climbed into the Blagden deer park" while hiking near Rock Creek.

Rock Creek "lake": adapted from USGS Washington West topographic map, 2014; Pelz Executive Mansion design, 1898: Library of Congress; Rock Creek tunnel map: *Washington Post* 5/23/1886; "Maryland Planners" 6/11/1959, "Cross-Park Freeway" 5/7/1959: *Evening Star*, reprinted with permission of the DC Public Library, *Star* Collection ©*Washington Post*; NCPPC map, 1930: National Park Service; Pope Lincoln Memorial design, 1912: National Archives; Murphy/Olmsted design for Lincoln Memorial Arch: *Washington Herald* 1/21/1912; Fawn: *Theodore Roosevelt's Letters to His Children*, Charles Scribner's Sons, 1919.

Z is for ZOO

As the movement to create Rock Creek Park was gaining momentum in the late 1880s, the Smithsonian needed a place to house dozens of wild animals the Institution brought to the Mall starting in 1887.

William Temple Hornaday (left), curator of the Smithsonian's newly established Department of Living Animals, acquired more than 170 mammals, birds and reptiles. Initially they were meant to be models for his fellow taxidermists. Then — alarmed at the near-extermination of the American buffalo — Hornaday envisioned the collection as the foundation for a national zoo that could save threatened species and educate the public. Visitors flocked to the grounds near the Smithsonian Castle to see the menagerie — from bison, bears and badgers to vultures, vipers and Virginia deer.

In March 1889, President Grover Cleveland signed a huge, catch-all appropriations bill. One section authorized a new home for the Smithsonian's animal collection — a National Zoological Park whose aim was "the advancement of science, the instruction and recreation of the people." A proposed amendment had called for the establishment of Rock Creek Park. But it failed, as park opponents supported the zoo as a less costly alternative. The park would have to wait for a new Congress.

Where Should the Wild Things Be

A zoo commission was charged with finding an appropriate location somewhere along Rock Creek between Massachusetts Avenue and Military Road. Among the sites considered was property around Peirce Mill. The commissioners selected a spot closer to the city, but similar in nature — rising above the creek in hills and plateaus near the site of a historic mill, a quarry and an old mansion. Among the property owners who gave up land for the zoo was Joshua Pierce Klingle, from the Peirce family.

Opened to the public in 1891, the zoological park was designed by landscape architect Frederick Law Olmsted (whose son, F. L. Olmsted Jr., would go on to shape the layout of Rock Creek Park). Animal enclosures were erected on the plateaus. The quarry road became the main path through the zoo (now called Olmsted Walk). The mansion, Holt House, was used as administrative offices until 1977. One of the zoo entrances is off Adams Mill Road, named for the mill.

From the arrival in 1891 of Dunk and Gold Dust — the zoo's first elephants — to the birth of giant pandas Tai Shan (2005), Bao Bao (2013) and Bei Bei (2015), Washingtonians have gone crazy for some of the

Established at nearly the same time, the National Zoo and Rock Creek Park share a common history, environment and mission.

Youngsters in the 1890s view the zoo's first bison (above). Early in the 20th century, visitors could get up close and personal with an orangutan (below). Today the orangutans travel above their heads on the O-Line (top of page). Also pictured at top: a bald eagle and the zoo's first surviving giant panda cub, Tai Shan.

zoo's animals. Soko, a chimpanzee acquired in 1915, would take walks about the grounds and pour milk from a bottle as he ate formal meals sitting at a table. Ham — the astronaut chimp whose 1961 launch paved the way for US manned spaceflight — retired from the Air Force and joined the zoo from 1963 to 1980. Smokey Bear — a cub that survived a New Mexico forest fire — lived at the zoo from 1950 until his death in 1976, serving as a symbol of the public service campaign against wildfires. Mohini, a white tigress, arrived in 1960. More recently, Rusty the red panda lit up Twitter in 2013 after escaping from his yard and making it all the way to the Adams Morgan neighborhood before being captured.

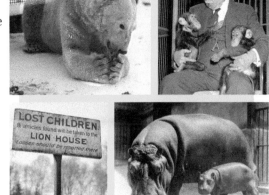

A New Zoo

The National Zoo entered its modern era in the 1950s and 60s, returning to Hornaday's original commitment to save endangered species and inform the public. For decades, the emphasis had been on exhibiting as many types of animals as possible. Now the zoo began transforming into a center for research, breeding and conservation of threatened species, where naturalistic displays can teach visitors about preserving

William Blackburne (top right) welcomes two six-month-old chimpanzees to the zoo in 1938. Blackburne became the zoo's first Head Keeper in 1892, retiring in 1943 without taking a day off for vacation or illness. Animals no longer exhibited at the zoo include polar bears (shown c.1920) and hippos (c.1933). Zoo officials said the sign posted in the 1940s reduced the number of lost children considerably.

these animals. In 1975, the zoo opened a separate research campus, now the Smithsonian Conservation Biology Institute, in Front Royal, VA. Since 2006, the zoo's newest habitats have included Asia Trail, Elephant Trails and American Trail — with plans for a new bird exhibit focused on migrating species in the Americas.

Part of the Neighborhood

The zoo has taken advantage of its setting in Rock Creek Valley, sheltered from the urban landscape around it. In the early years, the creek even served as a watering hole for the elephants. As in Rock Creek Park, New Deal agencies put unemployed Americans to work at the zoo during the 1930s, erecting the Small Mammal House and Reptile House and providing art throughout the grounds. The zoo's newest buildings support the valley's environment through sustainable design elements such as green roofs and geothermal heating and cooling. The zoo grounds also provide habitat for local wildlife. One of the most anticipated events each spring is the return of the black-crowned night herons to their nesting colony near the Bird House.

The National Zoo conducts research aimed at saving endangered animals, including such iconic species as Bengal tigers and giant pandas (above). Exhibits are designed to enlist the zoo's more than two million annual visitors in the conservation effort.

The zoo shares some of the same problems as the park, including traffic. Until 1966, the main paths through the zoo were for cars, and driving through the park to the zoo involved splashing through fords that became impassable after heavy rains. The overpopulation of deer has spilled over onto the zoo's campus — though one animal learned the hard way in 2013 not to jump into a cheetah yard.

The National Zoo and Rock Creek Park, created just 18 months apart, endure as neighbors and partners in preservation — protecting vulnerable species around the world and a treasured local wilderness.

Afterword

It takes more than one visit to appreciate what Rock Creek Park has to offer — and more than a single trip through the alphabet.

A complete list from A to Z of the park's living things would range from the Acadian flycatcher (a small, greenish migratory bird sometimes spotted during the spring and summer) to the Zebra swallowtail (a black-and-white striped butterfly found mainly near paw paw trees). A page for each of the nearly 1,200 species described by the National Park Service as "present" or "probably present" would produce a book close to three inches thick. In addition to plants and animals, the roster includes mushrooms and other fungi sporting colorful names like the Destroying Angel, the Devil's Urn, Chicken of the Woods and Eastern Cauliflower (right).

A single pass through the alphabet also leaves out historical trivia that can amaze or amuse:

- Lincoln assassin John Wilkes Booth made his getaway on a horse he hired on the pretext of going riding to a site now in Rock Creek Park.
- Joshua Peirce, who ran the family's successful 19th century nursery business, was not the only member of his family with a green thumb: his father's cousins in Pennsylvania established an arboretum that was the foundation for Longwood Gardens.
- Across the creek was the country home of Russia's eccentric ambassador to the United States. Alexander de Bodisco is most often remembered for his marriage at age 53 to a Georgetown teenager. However, he was one of Washington's favorite diplomats, and his grave overlooks Rock Creek in Oak Hill Cemetery.
- In the annals of the park, John Kennedy was a New York infantryman (buried at Battleground Cemetery after losing his life at the Battle of Fort Stevens) and Dolly Madison was a DC candy company (whose executive, Florence Blake, ran the teahouse at Peirce Mill from 1915 to 1919).

While the name Rock Creek has been appropriated for countless commercial ventures, it was the favorite soda for generations of locals. Rock Creek Beverages began in 1920 with a big tub of ginger ale — using water from the Potomac River, not the stream on the label.

As you explore Washington's wild wooded hills, what will you discover? Get out there and make some history of your own as you deepen your understanding of Rock Creek Park from A to Z.

Rock Creek Ginger Ale ad: *Evening Star* 4/6/1928, reprinted with permission of the DC Public Library, Star Collection ©*Washington Post*; Eastern cauliflower (top) and Runner south of Rapids Bridge (next page): David Swerdloff; Wood thrush (following page): Steve Maslowski, 2008, US Fish & Wildlife Service.

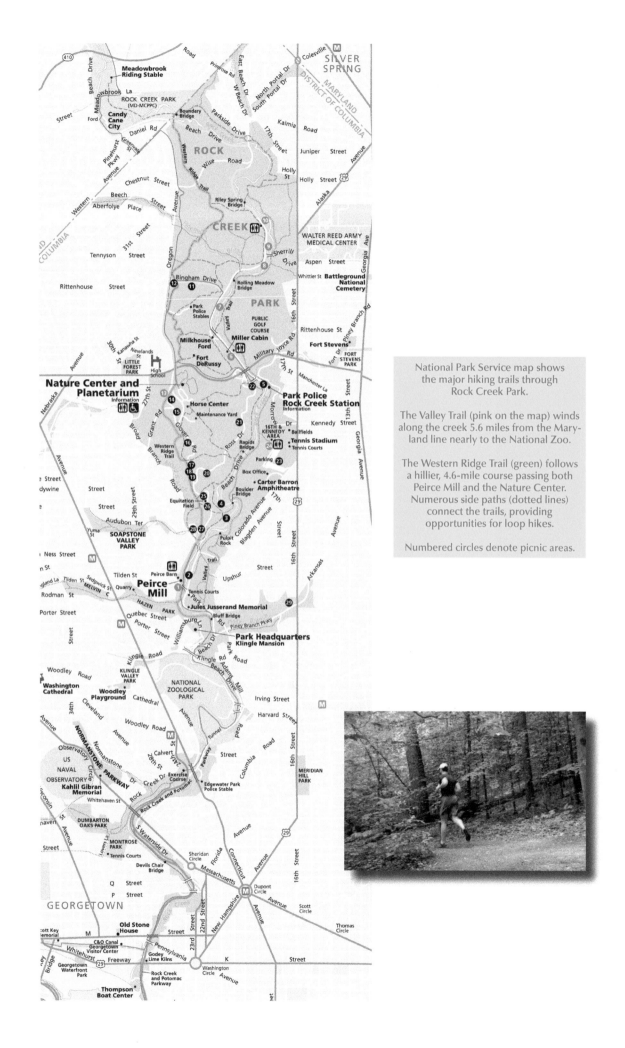

National Park Service map shows the major hiking trails through Rock Creek Park.

The Valley Trail (pink on the map) winds along the creek 5.6 miles from the Maryland line nearly to the National Zoo.

The Western Ridge Trail (green) follows a hillier, 4.6-mile course passing both Peirce Mill and the Nature Center. Numerous side paths (dotted lines) connect the trails, providing opportunities for loop hikes.

Numbered circles denote picnic areas.

The Wood Thrush
is the official bird
of Washington, DC.
Please support statehood
for the District of Columbia.